Hymnal Studies Four

Organ Planning
Asking the right questions
by John Fesperman

The Church Hymnal Corporation
800 Second Avenue, New York, New York 10017

Foreword

In the life of a congregation the purchase of a new pipe organ or the rebuilding of an old instrument is a very significant, if not, an historic event. This action presupposes an extended period of study by the priest and organ committee of the liturgical and musical needs of the congregation, the acoustics of the building and the physical properties of the space as they relate to the placement of the instrument and the choir. It also implies commitment of the congregation to a major financial investment.

Hymnal Studies Four: Organ Planning: Asking the Right Questions by John Fesperman is a very practical and stimulating guide for a congregation as it makes its crucial decisions on a new or rebuilt instrument. Mr. Fesperman, Curator of Musical Instruments at the Smithsonian Institution in Washington, D.C. and an active parish musician, approaches his subject by raising the important questions that must be wrestled with in a project of this magnitude. His book provides historic background on the development of the pipe organ and includes well illustrated information on its structure and action.

However, the qualities that set this book apart from others on the subject emanate from its focus on questions of the liturgical and theological appropriateness of a particular instrument for a specific congregation and place. What is it about the liturgy, or work of the people of God in a particular place that should determine the design and placement of an instrument? What are the theological questions about the appropriateness of the design and placement and the proper stewardship of the peoples' talents and financial resources? These questions are seldom asked by clergy and committees making decisions on organ design: however, they are essential to the process.

In Mr. Fesperman's writing we have wisdom, artistic and musical sensitivity coupled with profound liturgical and theological understanding. Under his guidance, probing, perceptive congregations can be led to the selection of an instrument that will be to the glory of God and the enrichment of the liturgical life of the community.

Raymond F. Glover

Acknowledgements

Writing for a general audience by one who is both a regular Sunday organist and a crusader for good instruments is a sobering assignment: while the organ is the most complicated of musical instruments, its makers and players often make its workings appear unnecessarily mysterious. While it is difficult to avoid the terms of the trade, it is important to make the instrument understandable for those charged with making decisions on behalf of parishes that must live with the results for many decades.

This book could hardly have been written without the generous help offered by many musicians, organ builders, clergy and others who have patiently responded to requests for advice and information. Barbara Owen's encyclopedic knowledge of American organ history has been invaluable and William Parsons of the Library of Congress has called attention to many publications which might otherwise have gone unnoticed. Gratitude is also due the Harvard University Press for permission to use drawings and to Marcia Tucker of the Smithsonian Institution, who made them.

Among those who have reviewed sections or otherwise provided advice and criticism, aside from organ builders, are the following: The Rev. Sherodd Albritton, Virginia Theological Seminary; Robert Anderson, Southern Methodist University; Catherine Bell, Grace Church, Washington; William Crane, St. Francis' Church, Potomac, Maryland; David Dahl, Christ Church, Tacoma; James S. Darling, Bruton Parish Church, Williamsburg; Carolyn Darr, Christ Church, Charlotte; John Ferris, Harvard University Memorial Church; Robert Finster, St. Luke's Church, San Antonio; Charles P. Fisher, Cambridge Records, Inc.; Thomas Foster, All Saints' Church, Beverly Hills; Joan Haggard, Music Commission, Diocese of Michigan; David Klepper, Klepper, Marshall and King, Inc; The Rev. Stephan Klingelhofer, Grace Church, Washington; Charles Krigbaum, Yale School of Music; Arthur Lawrence, *The American Organist*; James Litton, St. Bartholomew's Church, New York; Betty Louise Lumby, University of Montevallo; Douglas Major, Washington Cathedral; John Marsh, St. Martin's Church, Houston; Robert Moog, Big Briar, Inc.; the late

Robert Newman, Bolt, Beranek and Newman, Inc.; Richard Parsons III, Sunbury Press; William Peterson, Pomona College; John Renke, Grace Cathedral, San Francisco; Howard Ross, Church of the Transfiguration, Dallas; Robert Selim, Editor, National Museum of American History; Charles W. Thompson, Nashotah House; the Rev. John W. Turnbull, Grace Cathedral, San Francisco.

For the friendly advice and patient encouragement of Raymond F. Glover and Frank Hemlin of the Church Hymnal Corporation, I am especially grateful. Any errors of fact or judgement are of course my own.

JF
Washington, 1984.

"Music and silence — how I detest them both! We will make the whole universe a noise in the end."

THE SCREWTAPE LETTERS,
C. S. Lewis

Contents

❦

IV Planning a New Instrument

I Introduction

The organ and its music have been central to the liturgical life of the western church since renaissance times: reason enough to warrant careful consideration, not only by those who play, sing or listen, but especially by those who are responsible for planning new instruments.

Liturgical renewal has brought with it musical renewal and, as in earlier times, renewal invites more ardent and knowing participation by all. Making a joyful noise is the primary purpose of the organ, and this book aims to encourage all who find music an important part of their corporate religious life. To appropriate what is valid in traditional ways in light of contemporary needs is the point of its instructional sections.

The first purpose of this book is to explain in plain language and without undue technical detail what the traditional organ is and how it works. By "traditional" is meant the organ as it has been known in the western world for more than four centuries: in its most archetypal form with its inherently logical mechanical design. This is the instrument whose musical and mechanical validity have been rediscovered during the second half of the 20th century after the 19th century introduction of electric and pneumatic devices to its mechanical operation.

A second aim is to enable those with limited experience to ask the right questions when a new instrument is being planned. These objectives are treated in terms of instruments and buildings of moderate size where musical and liturgical needs are likely to be normal rather than extraordinary. By "moderate size" is meant an organ of not more than 25 stops and a building seating not more than 400.

A third purpose is to affirm that liturgical and theological integrity demand musical integrity. In the case of organs, this implies excellence in workmanship and design, however modest an instrument might be.

Hence, advice about organs is interspersed with observations about liturgy and the place of music in it. Underlying this is the conviction that the liturgy is concerned with every aspect of the lives of God's people. It is especially concerned with work and therefore with the vocations of all workers; in this case, specifically the calling of workers who make organs.

Such an approach requires that recommendations made here be in terms of an ideal solution. It is only when the ideal is clear that planners have a standard against which to measure decisions. When compromise is inescapable, it is best defined by those responsible for finding the best resolutions in light of all the factors in a given situation.

To speak in terms of the best possible musical and liturgical solution means that planners must also have an eye to the future. They must take into account new music for the organ and new ways of using music in the liturgy. The traditional organ has endured for centuries largely due to its ability to satisfy a wide range of liturgical and musical requirements: it is the most versatile of instruments.

Composition of important organ music has dwindled only in times when the traditional principles of organ building have been ignored. When the craft has fallen into confusion and disarray (as it did in the early twentieth century), so has the creation of music for the organ. Both the instrument and its earlier repertoire invite new music and new uses which can succeed only when the integrity of the instrument itself is respected.

Organ music played today spans more than five centuries. The instrument's versatility has consistently attracted the greatest of composers who have created for it a vast repertoire which continues to move modern hearers as it did those of earlier times. Much of this music has been preserved by the Church itself. This is due to its quality rather than its age, and especially because it includes settings of known hymn tunes ranging from traditional English folk melodies to the Lutheran chorale, the psalter tune and plainsong. Familiar examples are such durable tunes as *Greensleeves*, *A Mighty Fortress*, *Old Hundredth*, and *O Come, Emmanuel*. These and many others provide not only a basis for many organ pieces, but also for the organ's noblest task: support of congregational song.

Although much is said about organs themselves in these pages, no organ builders are recommended. Instead, the characteristics essential to the integrity of the instrument are described. The essential advice about choosing an organ builder is contained in this query: "Why do you make organs?" On the answer to that hangs the builder's chance to create an instrument worthy of use in the liturgy.

II Three Essentials of Organ History

To understand the present-day organ, it is necessary to have an acquaintance with at least the following three aspects of its development:

Liturgical music: liturgical instrument

The long association of the organ with liturgical worship has occasioned the composition of much music for liturgical use. By the time of Luther and Cranmer, the early sixteenth century, sophisticated organs were appearing throughout Europe. Their earliest repertoire was largely based on plainsong tunes from hymns and sections of the Mass.

The use of known church tunes as a basis for organ music has continued to the present day, reaching its zenith in the first half of the eighteenth century when the chorale preludes of J.S. Bach raised the Lutheran chorale to its most sublime point. In Roman Catholic cultures, much post-Reformation music continued to use plainsong tunes, producing such lasting and beautiful works as those of de Grigny and Couperin in France and Frescobaldi in Italy, among many others. Some of the most attractive keyboard music ever written is found in the dozens of books of variations on familiar French Christmas carols (*Noels*) composed during the seventeenth and eighteenth centuries and still a favorite part of the organ repertoire.

By the time the Pilgrims arrived in Plymouth in 1620, much organ music still played today was well known — the works of Praetorius in Germany, William Byrd in England, Titelouze in France, Arauxo in Spain, or Sweelinck in Holland. Each of these areas also produced organs of distinctive design suited to the music written for them.

The organ's ability to support congregational singing further secured its place in Lutheran Germany and later in Anglican countries as well. Congregational participation was one thing on which many reformers agreed. Even the Scotch and Swiss Calvinists, with their unaccompanied psalm tunes, eventually succumbed to the use of the organ to support them.

Neither organs nor even music itself have always been thought to enhance worship, even by some Anglicans. From the time of Archbishop Cranmer (whose allegiance to the Church of England cost him his life in 1556) through the Commonwealth (1649-1660), English liturgical and musical controversies can be described as a pitched battle, fought against "superstitious vanities, poperies and fooleries," as one Peter Smart described the goings on at Durham Cathedral in the 1620's. Many organs were destroyed, including the one in Westminster Abbey where "they [the soldiers] brake down the organs and pawned the pipes at several ale-houses for pots of ale."[1]

The English Pilgrims, who brought anti-musical views with them to the new world in 1620, saw to it that no organs were allowed in their houses of worship. Despite all this, organs soon appeared in American churches, with the Lutherans out-distancing the Anglicans for a time due to their regard for both the congregational chorale and instrumental music. The first organ for a church in New England went to King's Chapel, Boston in 1713, having been accepted as a gift by that Anglican congregation after having been declined by the puritan Brattle Square Church.[2]

Organ building: an ancient craft

European organ building was so well established by the mid-sixteenth century, that the theorist Michael Praetorius was able to describe a craft already musically and mechanically mature when his *Syntagma Musicum* was published in 1619. Instruments of the early seventeenth century produced sounds of a variety equal to that found in today's instruments. It is instructive to reflect that not one significant organ voice has appeared that was not already known and used in Europe before 1700. Such an historical perspective suggests that technological progress has little to do with artistic quality.

1. As cited in Le Huray, *Music and The Reformation in England*, (London: Cambridge University Press, 1978), pp. 48 and 54.
2. For a lively account of puritan opposition to organs, see Owen, *The Organ in New England*, p. 1, ff.

While many early organs are still in use in Europe, only a tiny percentage of those imported or made in the United States before 1850 still serve their congregations. They have disappeared, not because they have worn out, but because the American preoccupation with bigness as well as modernity caused them to be replaced again and again as congregations grew more affluent or more seduced by novelty. Three of the oldest that still provide music every Sunday may be seen in the Lutheran Church in Madison, Virginia, (1802) and in the Methodist and Unitarian churches on Nantucket Island, Massachusetts (both dated 1831). Beautiful organ cases, now only facades for later organs replacing those made in the eighteenth century, may be found in varying states of preservation in Christ Church, Boston; Christ Church, Philadelphia; St. Michael's Church, Charleston and elsewhere. It is to these few remnants that American builders now turn for a hint of the American musical past.

Amid wars and other disasters, the European tradition of organ building survived. It still sets a high standard for modern organ builders whose craft has changed little over the centuries.

Recent changes in American organ building

In the United States, traditional organ building was overwhelmed by rapid technological change in the late nineteenth and early twentieth centuries.

American builders moved away from traditional practices largely because they became enthralled with the new technology of electricity which made possible instruments of unlimited size. The pipes of the organ could now be put almost anywhere with the keyboards located almost anywhere else, connected only by a cable, rather than direct mechanical linkage.

The organ began to imitate the orchestra as epitomized by the theatre organs of the 1920's: wondrous machines indeed they were, but they were intended to accompany action in silent movies, rather than to support singing or play organ music. The organ's repertoire, much of which had liturgical origins, was often entirely overlooked in favor of spectacular sound effects of all sorts. Before the advent of the phonograph and later the radio, the great municipal auditoriums of the day boasted large organs. These were often used to play transcriptions of orchestral music for a large public, especially in towns where no orchestra was to be found. For a time, the craft of organ building became an industry racing to satisfy a ravenous market which included residence organs built for the very rich, often with automatic player mechanisms attached.

The *one man band* sort of instrument influenced other organs, notably those designed for churches. The use of electricity made it possible to install "antiphonal" divisions above ceilings or beneath floors. While church organs did not become identical to theater organs, sound from such distant locations often had to travel around obstructions or through small openings, with consequent loss of promptness and clarity. As it became possible to hear music of all kinds on records, and as other advances in communications technology occurred, the Great Depression also arrived. This halted much of the frenzied activity in the organ industry, and many builders were soon bankrupt.[1] While almost 2500 organs were built in 1927, only 479 were completed in 1935 and more than half of the organ firms had disappeared. In retrospect, it seems clear that artistic bankruptcy accompanied financial ruin.

Out of this chaos emerged two serious organ builders who sought to return the organ to its former position as a respectable musical instrument, able to play its own great repertoire once more. They were Walter Holtkamp in Cleveland and Donald Harrison, an English builder who had come to the Aeolian-Skinner Company in Boston. Their first concern was a musical one and they questioned innovation for its own sake; both were aware of the traditional organs still in use in Europe. It was to these that they turned for a basis for re-establishing the organ's identity in America. The revival of the old craft, which they began in the 1930's and 1940's, led further than even they might have predicted. Their work pointed the way for younger builders who proceeded to adopt more and more the traditional ways.

Holtkamp and Harrison fought hard for their musical convictions which are partly summarized by the following two public statements. Walter Holtkamp, speaking to the Music Teachers' National

---

1. For a fuller discussion of this time, see Ochse, *The History of The Organ in the United States*, pp. 343-366.

Association in 1940 observed, "That the American organ of the last generation failed to endure, I attribute very much to the fact that it was too complete a break with the past, and that not enough composition of an enduring nature appeared for it, to keep it alive as a new instrument."[2] Donald Harrison, discussing the then new Aeolian-Skinner organ in Harvard's Germanic Museum asserted, "As a result of its transformation into an imitation symphony orchestra, the organ not only lost its original character but has come to be frowned on by every musician not an organist."[3]

In 1933, Holtkamp constructed a Positive division for the Cleveland Museum of Art organ, and Harrison followed in 1936 with a new organ for Harvard's Germanic Museum. A renaissance in organ building in the United States began with these instruments. By the 1950's European organs, made in much the same way as organs of two centuries earlier, were being imported into the United States. During these years, a new generation of American builders was appearing, distinguished by their commitment to traditional instruments using mechanical rather than electric action.

In 1961, the first large instrument made in the old style by an American builder (the late Charles Fisk) was installed in Mount Calvary Church, Baltimore. Since that time, the number of shops building organs in the traditional way has increased rapidly. A recent survey[4] showed some fifty small firms in the United States devoted to construction of traditional instruments, whereas forty years earlier there were none. While these shops account for far less than half the total number of new organs made in the United States each year, their influence is out of proportion to their size, especially since many music schools and university chapels, as well as churches have acquired their organs for teaching and performance. Thus, a large percentage of the present generation of organists is well experienced in the use of such instruments and can be counted upon to prefer them.

The early years of the revival produced their share of failures too, largely because of a well-intentioned effort to reproduce traditional

2. "Present day trends in organ building," MTNA Proceedings, 1940.
3. As quoted in the *Christian Science Monitor*, Mar. 27, 1937.
4. In Pape, *The Tracker Organ Revival in America*, pp. 131, 132.

organs without fully understanding how. The result was, in some cases, "neo-baroque" instruments which were unsatisfactorily aggressive in sound, ungraceful in appearance or provided with clumsy actions. Good builders learn from mistakes and by 1970, most had learned to produce instruments characterized by full and free sound with light actions and handsome cases, based on a fuller understanding of earlier principles of design: American organ building had again come of age.

The preceding three glimpses of the development of the organ as a liturgical instrument, the traditional craft in Europe and its recent revival in the United States may well include more than planners of a new instrument want to hear. Such background should help them make decisions in as informed manner as possible. Books in the resource list will provide more information for those who wish to read further.

III The Traditional Organ

What makes up a traditional organ and how does it work?

The organ is a wind instrument controlled by one or more keyboards for hands and feet. The traditional organ has changed little over four centuries, although its identity has been partly obscured by short or long-lived innovations such as the application of electricity to its mechanical operation beginning in the late nineteenth century. It is most easily understood in its traditional form, which is the basis for the description which follows. (Drawings A and B, the Glossary and photographs should be consulted as needed.)

The simplest organ consists of a set of *pipes* (one for each note of the scale), resting on a *windchest*, to which air under pressure is supplied by a *bellows*. Each pipe sounds when an appropriate key is depressed, opening a valve to admit air to the foot of the pipe.

Most organs have several sets of pipes, called *stops*. Each set requires a *stop action* to allow one or more pipes to sound simultaneously. For example, if three stops are drawn, three pipes sound when the valve is opened by depressing the key.

The whole instrument is housed in one or more wooden cabinets called *cases*. The facade of the case displays the pipes for the main stop of the organ. All other pipes stand directly behind inside the case itself. An organ with 56 keys and five stops would have 280 pipes, of which only 56, belonging to the "Principal" stop, would appear in the facade.

Pipes

Organ pipes are of two sorts. *Flue* pipes, made of metal or wood, are constructed like penny whistles: air forced against a metal tongue causes it to vibrate. Metal pipes are usually cylindrical and may be open or closed at the top. Some varieties are tapered and some have small *chimnies* at the top; all of these configurations affect the quality of the sound. Wooden flue pipes are rectangular in cross section, open or closed at the top.

Pitch of all flue pipes is dictated by the length of the pipe: the longer the pipe the lower the pitch. The normal length for an open flue pipe at low C is 8 feet. The pipe for the C an octave higher is only 4 feet long, since pipe lengths halve at each octave; thus the top C pipe would be only 6 inches long. Flue pipes made of metal or wood constitute the majority of pipes in the organ.

Reed pipes are the other variety used in the organ. They generate sound by a vibrating thin metal blade or reed, functioning much as the reed in a clarinet mouthpiece. Their sounds are much more exotic and often more aggressive than those of flue pipes, and they add special color and brilliance to the organ's sound. The reed is contained in a *boot* at the foot of the pipe. The pipe itself is usually made of metal, occasionally of wood, and may be cylindrical, flared, tapered or of other more complicated shapes. As with flue pipes, the shape affects the quality of the sound.

Windchest

Made of wood and rectangular in shape, the windchest is exactly what its name implies: a chest filled with wind. The top of the windchest accommodates a series of small round holes, one for each pipe, so arranged that all the pipes for one note stand behind each other. There is a separate windchest for the pipes of each keyboard or *division* of the organ as well as for the Pedal. A second division may be referred to by a variety of names, including "Positive," "Choir," "Swell," "Echo," etc., depending on its function and its location.

Bellows

Wind under pressure is supplied to the windchest by one or more bellows originally pumped by hand. Hand-pumped bellows are still made, although they are now fitted with an electric blower allowing wind to be supplied either electrically or manually. A bellows of large capacity is essential to insure that the wind supply is both adequate and flexible.

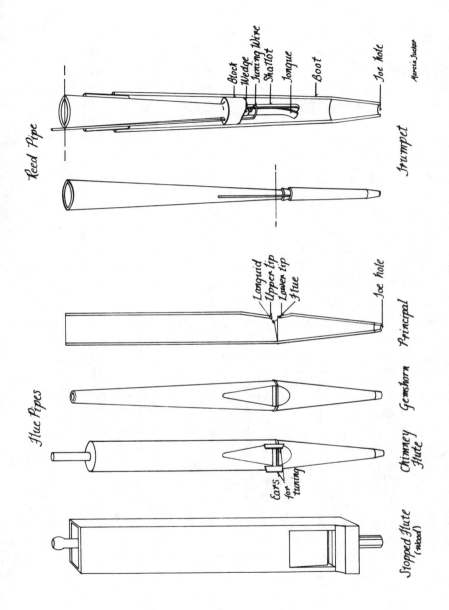

Drawing A: Organ pipes

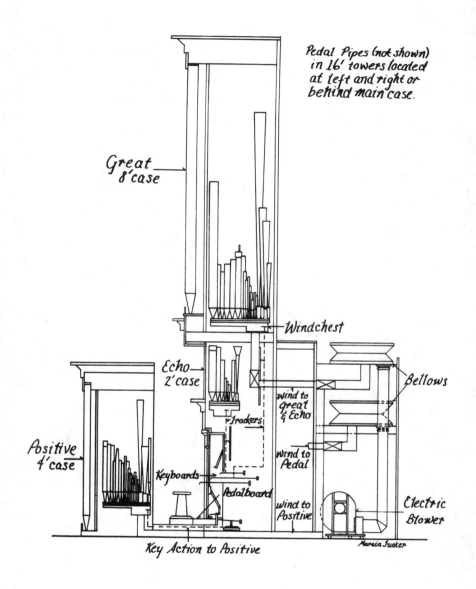

Pedal Pipes (not shown) in 16' towers located at left and right or behind main case.

Great 8'case

Windchest

Echo 2'case

Bellows

wind to great & Echo

Positive 4'case

Trackers

wind to Pedal

Keyboards

Pedalboard

wind to Positive

Electric Blower

Key Action to Positive

Marcia Tucker

Drawing B: Section through a three manual organ

Key action

Each key is connected to a valve (seated against the wind-channel under all the pipes for its note) by a wooden *tracker*. When the key is depressed, the valve opens admitting wind to blow the pipes. When the key is released, the valve is closed by a spring.

Stop action

So that the organist may use various sounds of the organ either singly or together, each set of pipes (or stop) is controlled separately by a knob which can quickly be placed in an on or off position. This knob is connected to a *slider* — a long, thin strip of wood which has holes matching those under the pipes; it slides from left to right, admitting or denying air to the pipes above.

Hence the organ, like the harpsichord, has two distinct actions: one for the keys and one for the stops.

Case

The pipes for each windchest of the traditional organ are housed in a separate wooden case. The case has several functions, not the least of which is to protect the pipework and mechanisms from dust. It reflects and blends the sound, focussing it through its open front so that it is projected in the direction of the listeners. An organ with two keyboards (and hence, two windchests) normally has two separate cases, often with one located above the other. Pipes for the pedal keyboard are often divided into two *tower* cases, located at the left and right of the main organ case. On occasion, pedal pipes are incorporated into the central case behind the windchest for the Great organ.

Because its shape and size are dictated by the size of the windchest inside, and because its sides support the heavy components of the organ, the case is an integral part of the instrument, not merely a decorative afterthought. Its facade, usually ornamented with carved pipe shades and other wood sculpture, normally displays the pipes for the main (literally called "Principal") stop of the division. Hence, the size and proportion of the case announce visually the size and function of the organ.

A well designed organ case has the virtue of being architecturally honest: it should match the scale of the building, with ornament appropriate to its surroundings and to its musical and liturgical function. Its honesty is further strengthened because it contains the keyboards at its center — the only location musically and mechanically logical for them.

What are its characteristic sounds?

Principal and Chorus

The organ is a wind instrument and its characteristic tone colors are similar but not identical to the wind choirs of the orchestra. It possesses three basic families of sound, generally called Principal, Flute and Reed. In all but the smallest instruments, stops from each family appear in each division of the organ (Great, Positive, Swell, Pedal, etc).

The most distinctive organ sounds are those belonging to the Principal family. These stops have open flue pipes made of metal; the main Principal stop normally has its pipes placed on the front of the windchest and therefore visible in the facade of the organ case. Each division of the organ is organized around a stop of this family. This means that the voicing of all the other stops is related in intensity and timbre to the Principal stop on each windchest. The name thus signifies the most important sound of the organ as well as a family of tone. The temperament (see page 18) for tuning the entire organ is initially set on the main Principal stop of the Great Division.

Stops of the Principal family appear at different pitches, usually an octave apart, with a higher pitched *Mixture* from the same tone family. When the available pitches are used together, the result is the traditional Principal Chorus (also called *Plein Jeu*), literally a chorus of four or more pipes sounding for each note. This is the full, bright sound familiar in the support of hymn singing, as well as in much organ music. It, more than any other sound, distinguishes the organ. The tonal finishing of the complete Principal Chorus elicits the greatest care from the organ builder because it is the nucleus of sound basic to all organ music.

The basic Principal stop of the Great, or main, division is normally of unison or 8' pitch; the basic Principal stop of the second (Positive) division may be an octave higher (4' pitch). Since the longest pipe for each of these stops is 8' or 4' long respectively, their length defines the height of the organ case for each division. Ideally the low C pipe for each of these Principal stops can be seen along with the others in the facade of each case.

Flute and Reed Voices

While Principal stops of various pitches give substantial variety, stops from the other two tone families, the Flutes and Reeds vastly increase the organ's versatility. These voices also appear at different pitches and there is great variety within each of the families.

Flute stops are made of wide scale flue pipes in contrast to the narrow scale Principal pipes. Flute pipes are often made of wood and usually are stopped at the top. They provide the smoother less aggressive sounds of the organ and appear under a great variety of names, for instance, "Flute," "Bourdon," "Stopped Diapason."

Reed stops are characteristically bright in sound and often loud. Their pipes, as explained above, are constructed quite differently from flue pipes. They also bear a confusing variety of names, ranging from "Trumpet" or "Oboe" to "Bombarde," depending on the quality of sound chosen.

The variety found in the three tone families and in the use of different pitches in each gives the organist a large pallette of color from which to make choices dictated by the style of the music and the resources of the organ.

The organ as wind instrument

Because the organ is a wind instrument — a fact often obscured by its size — it responds to the player as do other wind instruments. Large flue pipes take a great deal of wind (like a Tuba or Bass Trombone) and therefore speak more slowly than small pipes, which require (like the orchestral flute or recorder) smaller amounts of wind. Reed pipes, when well regulated, speak very promptly. These characteristics affect the organist's choice of stops as well as tempo and articulation.

Which tuning system and basic pitch?

The tuning system or *temperament* used for the organ is important because it affects the total sound of the instrument. *Equal* temperament is usually considered normal for modern keyboard instruments. However, it works less well for the organ than for instruments like the piano, whose sound dies away relatively quickly, while organ sound continues at the same level until the key is released. With equal temperament, all intervals sound relatively well in tune, but none (except the octave) are perfectly so. This slight "out-of-tuneness" is therefore more noticeable in organ music. The compromises in equal temperament tuning have the advantage, however, of making it easier to use complicated keys and harmonies.

Meantone tuning systems were universally used until recent times for all keyboard instruments. There are many varieties of meantone tuning, all of which favor some intervals over others for perfect tuning, while the less perfect ones sound more dissonant. Since composers — through the eighteenth century at least — intended these effects in their music, there is good reason to consider meantone tuning for the organ. Its added advantage is that, for many important chords, the precise in-tuneness is clearly identifiable and essential to the total success of the music.

The tuning system must be taken into account when an organ is designed. Changing later from equal to a meantone system can be a troublesome and expensive undertaking although changes among varieties of meantone are more easily made. The organ builder's advice should be carefully heard.

The basic pitch of the organ should also be carefully considered in advance. While standard pitch of A' sounding at 440 cycles per second is used for the piano, this is a relatively recent practice. There is good reason to consider a slightly lower pitch for organs, since this can affect favorably the scaling of the pipes and therefore, their sound. Again, the organ builder should be consulted before any decision is made. If the organ is to be used with instrumentalists who are not experienced with tunings other than those based on A' 440, this must be taken into consideration.

How does it differ from electric action organs?

In the traditional organ, the connection between keys and pipes is a direct mechanical one accomplished by balanced levers called trackers. With electric action, this connection is achieved by magnetic switches, often in combination with small pneumatic motors — hence electro-pneumatic action. This is the most obvious difference which leads to other equally important ones.

During the five decades preceding the revival of traditional organ building in the mid-twentieth century, American builders produced only electric and electro-pneumatic instruments. While such still outnumber traditional instruments in the United States, the return to the traditional craft has proceeded rapidly (See page 7). This shift from modern electrical technology back to traditional practices is understandably confusing to the uninitiated. Therefore, substantial space will be devoted to some of the differences and to the reasons for the shift.

Actions and windchests

Although recent developments such as solid state circuitry have changed facets of electric action design (especially within the organ console), both key action and stop action usually operate with the complicated switches and pneumatic devices mentioned above. This applies both to the opening of the valves under pipes and to turning a given stop off or on. Such actions require more moving parts and are more intricate than traditional mechanical connections.

In electric action windchests, the wind reaches the pipes in a different way, and there is a separate valve for each pipe rather than for each note of the keyboard. An electric action chest with five stops will have five times as many separate valves as a traditional slider chest with five stops. Therefore, it is possible to make traditional windchests smaller than electric action chests. Thus, the entire organ requires less space. The multiplicity of valves in an electric action chest is detrimental to unanimity of speech and to blend when several stops are used at once since several valves rather than a single one must open for each note.

It is possible to electrify a traditional chest, but this creates similar musical problems: players cannot open valves by their own finger pressure and at their own speed. Control ends with the closing of a switch. And the switch may be located anywhere, often many feet from the pipes themselves. This loss of tactile communication with the source of the sound causes the organist to play less rhythmically: the instrument becomes more remote and the music suffers. Dispensing with direct connection between player and instrument seems technically convenient, but it creates a serious and illogical musical limitation.

Placement and size

Another difference that appears to be an advantage, but turns out to be a liability, is that electric action does not require the organ to be designed and built as a unity. Since pipes and keys need be connected only by a cable, there is great temptation to scatter parts of the organ in illogical locations robbing the instrument of its coherence. Many arguments have been advanced for dispersal of components of the organ about the building: to make control of a choir easier or to provide lines of sight between clergy and musicians, for instance. Such dispersal is equivalent to placing the tenors in a transept, the sopranos in the apse and the basses elsewhere, with the conductor located in still another place. This makes musical nonsense. When it is applied to the organ, a technological menagerie rather than a musical instrument is the result.

Because it is so easy to employ, electric action also tempts builders to make organs unnecessarily large rather than to make the choices which are essential to relate the entire design to the space in which it is heard. This can lead to a careless eclecticism: the borrowing of tonal ideas from French, English, German, Spanish or other styles without the synthesis which produces a coherent instrument.

This is not to say that a judicious eclecticism, as interpreted by a mature builder, represents unacceptable compromise — especially in view of the catholicity of twentieth century musical practice. It does mean that an "all-purpose" electric action organ easily becomes unnecessarily large, justified only by variety. A well designed organ is characterized by variety in both pitch and timbre, without being either enormous or scattered about in unsatisfactory locations.

Another temptation associated with electric action organs is to load the consoles with gadgetry, to become preoccupied with combination actions and other "aids to registration."[1] If an instrument actually requires such means of control, it has either grown too large to be managed or registrations normal to the traditional organ have become unsuccessful due probably to bad placement of the organ itself. This forces the player to find sounds which are more complicated than need be so that the instrument itself gets in the way of the music, rather than facilitate its performance.

Control by player

If the player has difficulty controlling the instrument, music-making takes second place to copying with a machine. ". . . Imagine a violin with an electrically operated bow; or better yet, a pianoforte with electrical wires connecting the keys to the hammers, thereby enabling the player to remain on stage with his keyboard and pedals, while the rest of the instrument might be elevated above the heads of the audience, quite out of sight, connected only by a cable. Fanciful and foolish as it seems, this was precisely the plight of the organ. As soon as electricity made possible the physical disembodiment of the organ's functioning parts, persuasive argument appeared for doing the surgery. Architects were quite comfortable removing the instrument's increasing bulk to enclosures and chambers, while leaving the player and console in view . . ."[2]

Maintenance and durability

Aside from musical matters, there is the problem of higher maintenance costs for electric action instruments than for traditional organs. Expensive action parts require periodic replacement, especially those involving leather or synthetic fabrics. The situation with such an instrument in Harvard University's Appleton Chapel is by no means unique. The University Organist and Choirmaster described the report of a committee, commissioned to recommend a solution, as follows: "After a thorough investigation, these experts in a Report to the President, June, 1960, advised against investing the

1. See glossary.
2. Fenner Douglass in *The Benjamin N. Duke Memorial*, p. 15.

necessary funds to releather the old instrument, unsatisfactory as it was, only to be faced with the same problem in another twenty-five or thirty years.

"The Committee recommended a new organ considerably smaller in size and placed in direct line of sight of the congregation. Such an instrument would be designed according to classic principles and would make use of mechanical action rather than electric action, a type of organ less costly to maintain and one which would not require expensive periodic releathering . . ."[3]

A similar conclusion was reached by the Chapel Renovation Committee of Duke University. Speaking of deciding whether to rebuild the electric action organ in the university chapel or replace it, James Ferguson noted: "Since both these alternatives were costly, serious consideration was given to each, with the conclusion that rebuilding would be at best a holding action for a period of about thirty years."[4]

Fenner Douglass, looking back over the period when many European organs were imported and American builders were re-learning the traditional craft, observes: "We now have proof that twenty year old tracker organs built by Flentrop can be as good as new, while the electro-pneumatic instruments of the same time have failed. On the basis of these models of craftsmanship and their superb performance, much progress has been made in a native industry."[5]

Electric action organs, in the hands of master builders such as Walter Holtkamp and Donald Harrison, achieved a high degree of perfection. It is the writer's contention that these builders brought their art to a point of no return because the ultimate objectives they intuitively sought turned out to be best realized by a whole-hearted return to traditional organ building. Ultimately, the best in electric action organ design sought to duplicate the traditional organ, hoping to dispense with its limitations: but those limitations are what, in fact, give the

3. In *The Isham Memorial Organ*, (Cambridge, MA: Harvard University, January 1968).
4. In *Benjamin N. Duke Memorial*, p. 13.
5. In *Flentrop in America*, (Raleigh NC: Sunbury Press, 1982), p. xv.

organ identity. To revive the traditional art, seen in terms of twentieth century needs, is the task which has fallen to their successors, the present generation of builders.

Since so many electric action organs are in use, the foregoing observations about their musical and technological validity are indeed unsettling. They are set forth here to encourage planners of new instruments to make decisions which will affect liturgical and musical life in their parishes for many years to come only after careful consideration of what an organ at its best really can be. As stewards, their charge is to make the best possible use of the parish's resources.

What about electronic instruments?

New sounds and imitations

The public has good reason to be confused by the plethora of electronic instruments now available. They are aggressively advertised and offered at every turn, from supermarkets to department stores and music shops. And electronic organs were by no means the earliest such instruments to appear.

Since the invention of the Theremin in 1920, a bewildering variety of devices, using various electronic means for generating sound, has been introduced. Their distinctive musical identity lies in their ability to produce new sounds and to provide new means for precise control of pitch, volume, timbre and rhythm, rather than to imitate traditional instruments. Their potential for artistic expression has elicited lively interest from composers — so much so, that most music schools provide electronic studios for instruction and experimentation.

Electronic keyboard instruments have been skillfully used in musical theatre and by popular ensembles, usually without the intent of suggesting sound of traditional acoustic instruments. The basic excitement arises from authentically new ways of creating and controlling non-imitative sounds. Such an approach has established its own idiom, with its own integrity.

The electronic imitation of the organ is quite a different matter. Here the aim is the duplication of traditional sounds. Moreover, recent use of digital computers makes possible more convincing imitation than was feasible with earlier analogue circuitry.[1] Nonetheless, there are both musical and technical problems. Natural musical sound is characterized by slight imperfections which vary unpredictably, making precise imitation risky at best. The flesh and blood character of natural sounds, beginning with the human voice, constitutes an ineffable appeal so that attempted copying leads to results that are in important respects always sterile. For one thing, utter predictability becomes boring. This is a kind of musical literalism which fails because it tries to copy exactly sounds whose appeal derives from their spontaneity. Natural sounds are never exactly the same. Just as a live performance differs from a recording, so does a slightly unpredictable natural sound differ from its imitation. Scientifically accurate reproduction misses the point altogether.

It is not the fidelity of the imitation, which can often be convincing to the inexperienced, that is important here. Nor are the matters of cost, durability or quality of workmanship at issue. The issue is the replacement of the genuine article with an imitation.

The decision to acquire an imitation of a real organ is often based on a misguided desire to be "traditional." This is, nonetheless, the antithesis of the Church's traditional regard for honesty. It amounts to trusting in appearances without substance. Being on the lookout for the inexpensive or the expeditious may be prudent so long as it is not at the expense of quality. The real issue is the integrity of the organ itself.

Edward Sovik, an architect much involved with church design, puts the matter unambiguously: "But the electronic imitation of the pipe organ, which is sometimes so good an imitation that a [layperson] can't distinguish it from the real thing, is another matter. That it is the product of ingenuity and great skill and that it is somewhat less expensive than a pipe organ makes it attractive, but these attractions don't change the fact that it is a phony imitation."[2]

The Musical Instruments Market

The production and merchandising of a variety of electronic instruments are associated with a large industry in which competition is fierce. Because of the nature of the products and the volume of business, dealers rather than makers negotiate with clients. A parish planning a new organ will be fair game for sales campaigns armed with promotional material and quick answers to questions about cost, delivery times, maintenance, space requirements and the like.

Although smaller electronic organs are relatively inexpensive to buy, more elaborate installations approach the cost of a traditional organ of eight to twelve stops. Even a modest instrument by a good builder can be so designed that it can serve in a large space and offer remarkable variety of sound. Both loudness and quality of sound have nothing to do with size of traditional organs. It is the quality of the organ rather than its size which calls forth the best efforts of the organist.

It is not inevitable that a real organ must cost more than its imitation, especially if the long range is taken into account. A survey comparing costs for purchase and maintenance of electronic and pipe organs concludes, "A church purchasing a pipe organ at this time [1976] will save money over the electronic within a twenty year period, assuming even a 'low' rate of inflation. In other words, it can spend as much as three times the cost of an electronic initially and still come out ahead in the long run."[3]

Marion Hatchett questions the durability of electronic organs: "In many ways the least satisfactory and, in the end, the most expensive substitute for an organ or a piano is an electronic instrument . . . . the lifetime of these instruments is that of any normal electric appliance, whereas a real pipe organ, though more expensive initially, can be expected to last through many decades. In fact, pipe organs have been known to last through centuries, given reasonable care."[4]

Two Canadian organ builders put the matter firmly: "Perhaps we cannot expect all members of organ committees to have the specialized knowledge to evaluate the musical resources of the three different kinds of organ [the traditional organ, electric action and electronic organs]. But we might expect of them the common sense to make sound long-range investments. Does anyone *invest* in a fake fur coat or put savings into costume jewelry? . . ."[5]

The musical instruments market envisioned by manufacturers has been aptly described in the press: " . . . Unlike traditional musical instruments, where sound is created by human actions — the drawing of a bow across a string, for instance — electronic sonics produce music by computer processing of information on silicon chips. Manipulating information is what computers are good at and that's what has made the musical instrument market a natural for consumer electronic companies to explore . . ."[6]

Changes in technology: imitation and obsolescence

Commercial pressures aside, electronic instruments have attracted serious musical attention because they point to an important expansion of musical resources. To predict that authentic electronic sound might not find legitimate liturgical uses would be foolish. That it will have its place alongside traditional musical activity, without presuming to replace it, is far more likely. In such a case, electronic sound is itself the *real thing*, shorn of inhibition inherent in imitation of traditional organ sound.

Further, the development of electronic musical media is only beginning. Rapid changes in technology raise the sobering thought that imitative organs may soon be rendered obsolete by more sophisticated approaches to the whole new resource. This brings up the question of whether spare parts and repairs will be available for out-of-date models in the foreseeable future.

Even the traditional keyboard may eventually be found inadequate for the still-evolving electronic resources. According to Robert Moog, a pioneer in the development of electronic musical instrument design: "Electronic instrument control interfaces designed to fully exploit the capabilities of a musician's hands will undoubtedly supplant the simple keyboards and controls of today's synthesizers."[7] Elsewhere, Moog, predicting the state of electronic music fifty years hence, looks back at attempts to imitate acoustical instruments as a practice to be "outgrown" by musicians: "At the beginning of the latter half of the twentieth century, musicians were preoccupied with the aesthetic problems of combining electronic and acoustic sounds, and instrument builders were preoccupied with making electronic instruments that accurately simulated the tone colors of acoustic instruments. Fortunately, musicians outgrew these concerns when they discovered that the electronic music medium, properly controlled, enabled musicians to impart as much subtlety and nuance to electronic sound as they could with acoustic sound. Today, of course, electronic musicians are deeply engrossed in the aesthetics and psychoacoustics of new synthesized sound, and understand that acoustic instruments have unique timbres and response modes which have evolved to a high state of perfection."[8]

Given his eminence in the field, Moog's warning is to be taken seriously: the imitating of traditional instruments may well be only a step on the way to more satisfying electronic sound. If so, the days of electronic organs are numbered.

Liturgy and musical integrity

What has the liturgical use of the organ to do with all this? The point is that the liturgy is concerned with the genuine and that the intent to deceive by imitation is unworthy of it. In the objects used, as in the preaching of the celebrant, the integrity of the liturgy demands authenticity in all its parts, including musical instruments. They need not be elaborate or extravagant — only genuine. This statement is more radical than it sounds because it takes for granted the religious conviction that all work is by nature sacramental, and, therefore, we dare not waste human energy in fabricating the cheap or the false.

"That all things be made new" applies to good liturgy, including its music. To use genuinely new creations responsibly is also to avoid using them merely as counterfeits.

1. For a technical discussion, see Junor, R., "The Electronic Organ" and Phelps, L., "The Third Kind of Organ," *Diapason,* March, 1983.

2. In *Architecture for Worship,* Augsburg: Minneapolis, 1973, p. 97.

3. "Keyboard Instruments in Worship," *Sacred Music,* Vol. 103, No. 3, Fall 1976, pp. 11 ff.

4. In *A Manual For Clergy and Church Musicians,* p. 41.

5. James Louder and Helmuth Wolff in "Future Trends," *The Tracker Organ Revival In America,* p. 84.

6. Michael Schrage in the business section of the *Washington Post,* May 3, 1983.

7. In "Electronic Music," *Journal Of The Audio Engineering Society,* Oct./Nov., 1977, p. 861.

8. In "Day of the Instrument Interface," *Music Journal,* Nov. 1976, p. 56.

IV   Planning a New Instrument

Why have an organ?

Reviewing musical and liturgical needs

The first question planners should ask themselves is "Why have an organ?" It is at least possible that such an instrument is not required: certainly vital religious communities exist without organs. Even when a congregation is sure it wants one, present and future liturgical and musical needs ought to be reviewed before the organ itself can be wisely considered. The objective is to define the optimum relation within a given parish between liturgical worship and music. Such a review should also consider the availability of a qualified person to play the new instrument and the willingness of the parish to commit funds, if necessary, for training an organist.

While significant commitments of time, energy and money are required to provide the best instrument for a given situation, planners should remember that a well made organ lasts for centuries rather than decades. If musical and liturgical activities are at a low ebb when they begin, a new organ can become a strong force for renewal. It can help raise future standards, rather than comply with a lower level of quality. Even if someone must be taught to play, it is certain that a good organ will attract good musicians in the future.

Function of a musical instrument

To ask, "Why have an organ?" means that planners must be clear about what the organ really is: a complicated musical instrument embodying craftsmanship of many different sorts. As a musical instrument, it has limitations; it is also versatile and colorful. Its limitations are that it is not a sound effects machine, nor is it an orchestra. Its versatility allows it to support congregational singing in inviting ways and to perform a variety of organ music even though it may be of modest proportions.

Liturgical and musical participation

"Why have an organ?" A good instrument, well played, enhances liturgy by encouraging congregational participation as well as by providing other music in the service. Regular hearing of a good instrument has a cumulative effect, often subtly, sometimes with great clarity. As experience widens, those with ears to hear will find an increasing ability to respond not only to music and sound, but to the ineffable contribution that any great artistic achievement makes to worship.

"Why have an organ?" Why have stained glass, sculpture or even a carefully designed building? None of these are ends in themselves and certainly ostentation must be distinguished from eloquence. A beautifully made musical instrument, like other liturgical objects, has value in the eyes of religious people because it represents the best work of human hands. When this knowledge becomes palpable in the liturgy, worshipers become aware that respect for work well done has meaning. They are reminded that work is a sacramental activity, a manifestation of Creation in the everyday world. St. Paul tells the Corinthians, "We are God's fellow workers . . ." and Christians respond, "Of thine own have we given thee."

The association of the organ with the church is a venerable one; it has been a stabilizing musical force in times of change. The organ is almost automatically associated with liturgical worship and for good reason: it surrounds hearers with sound of great variety and power and possesses a timeless repertoire of music based on known church tunes. The organ serves well because it is a genuine musical instrument well suited to its function. It is not more sacred than other instruments, nor are the latter more secular. Any instrument is made holy, not by the blessing of the Bishop, but by the integrity of the flesh and blood craftsmanship which created it.

How important is craftsmanship?

Integrity in workmanship

Integrity of workmanship is crucial for any object intended for liturgical use. This must be the point of departure because the essence of the liturgy bespeaks respect for all human work. While this book is concerned with the work of organ builders whose diverse skills make them an apt study in craftsmanship, it goes without saying that respect for work well done extends to the work of all people — be they plumbers, preachers, architects, cooks, musicians or janitors. It is when this conviction is watered down that the second-rate is tolerated in churches. When craftsmen sense that their work is not taken seriously, their regard for organized religion is understandably apprehensive. It is the Church's tolerance for inferior work which has cost it the allegiance of many who work with their hands. How can they feel welcome if their calling is regarded as either trivial or expendable?

The observations which follow aim to clarify why concern for good workmanship is essential to making responsible decisions when an organ is planned.

First of all, any temptations to be pretentious or ostentatious must be eliminated. Better a well-made, smaller instrument than an inferior larger one, no matter how imposing the facade.

Sacred and secular

The false distinction between sacred and secular must be avoided. Christians often limit their scope to what they have been taught to regard as sacred work, meaning thereby only what is done in or for churches. Nowhere is the artificial wall between sacred and secular more pernicious than when applied to the arts. It causes confusion and clouds judgement; worst of all, it tends to equate piety with competence. Such categories simply won't wash: " . . . there is no such thing as secular work. All work is sacred. Any activity which cannot be viewed in this light is probably something which should not be done at all."[1]

Madeleine L'Engle echoes a similar conviction: "Basically, there can be no categories such as religious art and secular art, because all true art is incarnational and therefore religious."[2] And finally, Dorothy Sayers

1. The Rev. Ruth T. Barhouse, in a sermon at St. Columba's Church, Washington, DC, January 27, 1980.
2. In *Walking on Water*, p. 25, Bantam, New York: 1982.

sums it up, when she writes that each person ". . . must be able to serve God in his work, and the work itself must be accepted as the medium of divine creation . . ."[3]

Paying for good work

Good workmanship must be honestly paid for. Much that is cheap or tawdry in churches is excused, not by lack of discrimination or taste, but by the claim that money is better spent on other things. To insist on careful workmanship is no extravagance so long as decency and order, rather than impressiveness, inform those who make such decisions. (Lots of churches with first-rate kitchen facilities have second-rate musical instruments!) "That money could have been given to the poor, of course," observed Clement Welsh, speaking of Washington Cathedral. "But this is the incarnational fact, the *principle of embodiment*, the mystery of the location of mind in brain, of beauty in the brushing of chemicals on cloth, of love in the embrace of bodies, of the Spirit in a little company of believers gathered in a building somewhere that is afflicted with years of deferred maintenance. To ask why, is to ask why we have this kind of a universe."[4]

An inferior or cheaply made organ results from work which "Shouldn't be done at all." It is not sanctified by liturgical use but by the quality of the vocations of the workers who made it. Bad workmanship is an insult to all who are called to be craftsmen, whether they make organs, chairs, stoves or buildings.

Those charged with commissioning a new organ have a special privilege: a sustained exposure to people whose calling is to make with their own hands a useful, durable, handsome thing whose purpose is to delight and inspire others. Such exposure can be profoundly illuminating because it exposes the gulf separating the genuine from the fake, the second-rate from the excellent. This distinction in a society permeated with advertising and hyperbole is always in danger

3. In "Why Work?", p.58. From *Creed or Chaos and other Essays*, Methuen, London: 1947 and 1954.

4. In a sermon preached at Washington Cathedral, June 7, 1980.

of being lost. Such a loss would be unendurable: with it goes the ability to identify the genuine, to be replaced by a callous attitude to all work and a loss of the religious concept of vocation itself.

There is a parallel concern, which is to consider all created objects as expendable or frivolous appendages to worship. Through the eyes of faith, such things are seen as yet more evidence of the sacramental in the communal life of all workers, all of whom suffer when a part is demeaned. Here again is the "incarnational fact," the chance to respond to Creation embodied in the work of others.

Work and Vocation

What does this theological undergirding mean for those who plan for a new organ? The question to ask is, "Is it well made," rather than only, "How much does it cost?" Of course, organ builders should be prepared to answer all manner of practical questions: With whom did you apprentice and for how long? Do you make your own pipes, keyboards and casework, or do they come from a supplier? Who does the carving for the case ornaments? What are you prepared to do, if some part of the organ does not function well? Good builders will have satisfactory answers to such questions because they attach their names to their work. A fine musical instrument is never anonymous, but quite literally part of its maker's life: a creation of flesh and blood, an offering of praise.

Through its use in the liturgy where the work of all people is offered, the organ becomes part of the life of the worshipping community. If the Incarnation is in fact seen in people and their work, then the highest purpose in making an organ is to return thanks for it.

A word about technology

A musical instrument is a work of art. Its integrity is directly related to the care taken by its maker in every detail, even allowing for occasional use of modern materials. While facsimiles of instruments can be turned out by mass production, no one equates a mail-order violin with a Stradivari, or with the work of humbler craftsmen, for that matter, so long as the work is good. Even in a large piano house, such as that of Steinway, much is always made of the handwork which is lavished on each instrument.

Modern technology is often admired because it has made the production of all manner of things so easy. There are obviously countless instances where technological change has produced incalculable benefit, from the washing of clothes to the saving of human life itself. But, in the realm of craftsmanship, its contribution remains subsidiary to the work of human hands. When it comes to organ building, in which intricate mechanisms play such an important role, the innocent observer might conclude that here assembly line methods should provide the perfect answer. Not so! While any responsible builder strives for efficiency, this is not to be confused with uniformity. The object is not to produce a line of indistinguishable instruments, but to give a special character to each.

It is true that a durable organ can be assembled with parts from supply houses. However, such an instrument can never perform in the same way as a carefully crafted organ. Any genuine work of art has its own ineffable character — even though it may not be noticed by everyone who hears it. A fine organ, like a great violin, is always attended by an air of mystery. Not even builders themselves can always say just why each instrument has its own personality. This may be partly explained by the care which handwork requires, but there is more to it than that. Each instrument made in a venerable tradition by human hands is also a new creation. Nothing precisely like it will ever appear again.

Technology in the emergency room or the air terminal, by all means! But let its limits be understood. To exceed them is to misuse technology itself by demanding results which are alien to it.

How big an organ and how much space is needed?

Relation to building

The size of an organ, both architecturally and tonally, must be carefully matched to the space in which it is seen and heard. It should be in scale with its surroundings in sound and appearance; this applies as much to the scaling and voicing of the pipes as it does to their number. A small organ can be quite loud and a larger one can be quite restrained: an organ designed for a small building would be quite differently scaled and voiced than an organ of the same number of stops intended for a larger or more reverberant space. Both acoustics and cubic volume are critical.

The size of the space in which the organ is used also influences the choice of the main Principal stop for each division, both as to pitch and intensity. This is a technical matter for the builder to decide — for instance, whether the Great or main division should be based on a Principal stop of unison pitch or on one an octave lower or higher.

Height is an important consideration since an organ based on a unison (8′) open Principal requires a low C pipe which is eight feet long. In a larger building, the basic pitch might be an octave lower (16′), requiring the longest pipe to have a length of sixteen feet and changing height requirements drastically. The total height needed for the case at its highest point in an organ based on an 8′ stop approaches sixteen feet since space must be allowed for windchests and keyboards underneath, as well as for cornices or other ornament at the top of the case. Should the main division be based on an open 16′ stop, twenty-five feet should be allowed for height.

Floor space is equally important, of course. An organ with two cases (one for the Great and one for the Positive) requires slightly more floor space than one in which one division is placed above the other. The normal location for the second case is at the gallery rail, so that some of its area, usually most of it, does not require floor space but is outside the gallery itself. Builders can give precise dimensions after they have investigated the space in which the organ will be placed and heard.

Optimum musical size

Small organs with only one keyboard are much more versatile than most people imagine. When well designed, they need not lack for volume and a great deal of excellent music exists for such instruments. If space and funds are limited, this need not preclude music-making of a very high order. It is far better to have a small organ in a small room than to force a larger one into an inhospitable space.

A small organ of two keyboards and pedal, with 10 stops or less, provides more musical flexibility than a single keyboard instrument and can play a larger segment of the repertoire. Any good small organ can certainly support congregational singing since volume is unrelated to size. In the hands of a skilled player, variety of sound belies the size of a modest instrument.

Well designed traditional organs take surprisingly small amounts of square footage. An organ of 15 to 20 stops should require floor space of approximately 8' by 4' for the main division; if the pipes and windchest for the second division are located above the main case, additional space is required only for the Pedal division. The Pedal may be incorporated into the main case, adding approximately two feet to its depth or placed in two side "tower" cases measuring about 4' by 3' each. The wind supply (including the blower) can be located inside the main case underneath the windchest.

If the chest and pipes for the second keyboard are located in a separate case, it is normally placed behind the player, overhanging from the front of the organ gallery. Its total floor space requirement will be less than its area (approximately 3' by 6') because of the overhang. All of these suggested measurements apply to traditional organs with mechanical action and slider windchests which can be designed very compactly. In the case of electric action organs, space requirements increase and there is also the temptation to design less efficiently since the action does not require that different parts of the organ be conceived as a unity (See page 19).

How large is too large? There are probably more instances of over-sized organs being forced into small spaces than vice-versa. In a small church, especially if ceiling height is low, an organ based on an open 16' stop is clearly inappropriate both visually and acoustically. While larger instruments give even more variety, an organ of 15 to 20 stops is adequate for churches of moderate size, providing for versatile support of congregational singing and for playing a great deal of organ repertoire. Except in buildings of cathedral proportions, an organ larger than 35 stops and three keyboards and pedal is inappropriate no matter how much money is available!

Proportion and pretension

The temptation to pretension can be great when a new organ is contemplated, and good liturgy is compromised by pretentiousness in music, as in other areas. The art of the wood sculptor is nonetheless essential in ornamenting the facade of the organ case since the organ is both an elegant and eloquent instrument. The important pitfall to avoid is redundancy within the organ's musical resources which are reflected in the size and proportions of the case.

List of Illustrations

Pictures have been assembled to show different solutions for case designs and for the placement of organ and choir. The instruments shown constitute only a sampling of recent work by American builders, scattered in various parts of the United States, to provide an indication of what is available to those who wish to visit parishes with traditional organs. While only American organs are shown here, many fine instruments imported from Canada and Europe also exist in this country.

Two drawings are included to show examples of organ pipes and mechanisms and for use with sections of the text in which they are described.

Plates

Plate 1

Two manuals and pedal, 14 stops, with a swell.
Placed at right side, east wall. St. Andrew's Church, Ojai, California.
MANUEL ROSALES, LOS ANGELES, 1983.   *Photo, Jim Lewis, Pasadena.*

Plate 2

One manual and pedal, 8 stops.
Placed on west wall beneath rose window. Trinity Church,
Collinsville, Connecticut.

C.B. FISK, CLOUCESTER, MASSACHUSETTS, 1971.

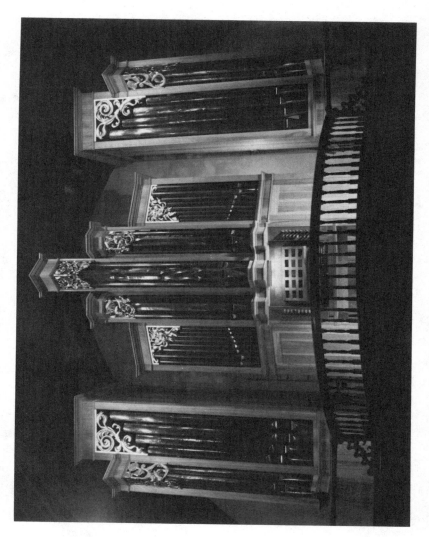

Plate 3

Two manuals and pedal, 17 stops.
Placed in west gallery, pedal pipes in towers to left and right. Grace
Church, Washington, D.C.
DAVID MOORE AND CO., NORTH POMFRET, VERMONT, 1981.

Plate 4

Two manuals, 14 stops (the lower keyboard couples the two upper ones).
Placed against west wall. St. Barnabas Church, DeLand, Florida.
VISSER-ROWLAND ASSOCIATES, HOUSTON, 1982.

Plate 5

Two manuals and pedal, 26 stops, with a swell.
Placed behind free-standing altar at east end of nave. St. Paul's Church,
Brookline, Massachusetts.

GEORGE BOZEMAN, JR. AND CO., DEERFIELD, NEW HAMPSHIRE, 1982.
Photo, Hutchins.

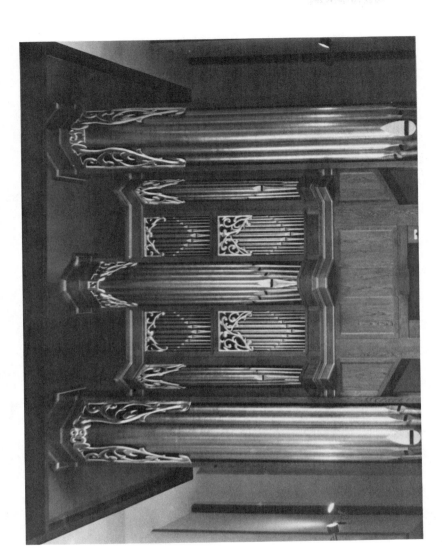

Plate 6

Two manuals and pedal, 7 stops.
Placed in the west gallery, with bass pipes of open Principal 16′ in side towers. St. Mark's Chapel, University of Nebraska, Lincoln.
GENE R. BEDIENT COMPANY, LINCOLN, NEBRASKA, 1981.

Plate 7

Two manuals and pedal, 13 stops, with a swell.
Placed on east wall to right of altar. Christ Church, Albion, New York.
ANDOVER ORGAN COMPANY, METHUEN, MASSACHUSETTS, 1979; *rebuilt
from a Steere & Turner organ 1873, retaining old case.*

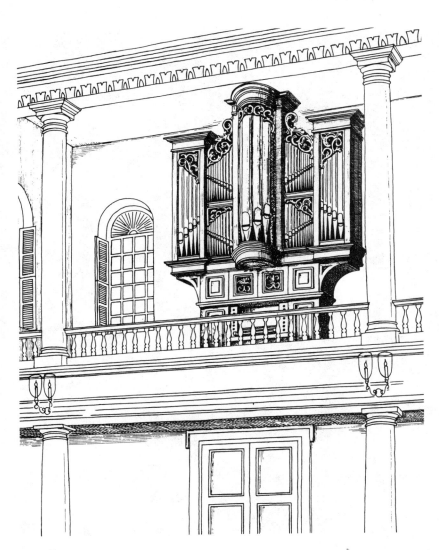

Plate 8
Two manuals and pedal, 17 stops.
Placed in west gallery. St. Helena's Church, Beaufort, South Carolina.
TAYLOR AND BOODY ORGANBUILDERS, STAUNTON, VIRGINIA, *under construction*, 1984.

Plate 9

Two manuals and pedal, 13 stops.
Stop action visible at right; pedal pipes at left. Church of the
Transfiguration, Dallas, Texas.
ROBERT SIPE, INC., DALLAS, 1973.

Plate 10

Two manuals and pedal, 13 stops.
Placed in the west gallery with a separate Positive case at the gallery front. Pohick Church, Lorton, Virginia.

NOACK ORGAN COMPANY, GEORGETOWN, MASSACHUSETTS, 1968.

Plate 11

Two manuals and pedal, 21 stops.
Placed against west wall. Christ Church, Tacoma, Washington.
JOHN BROMBAUGH AND ASSOCIATES, EUGENE, OREGON, 1979.
Photo, William Van Pelt.

Erik Routley, speaking of architecture, with obvious implications for other liturgical considerations, defines the danger inherent in ostentation: " . . . Pretentiousness implies that behind the facade there is an insufficient backing of truth and honor. In practice, it implies a combination of large and impressive size with cheap materials, and with an implied contempt for craftsmanship."[1]

What is the best location for an organ?

Sound projection and liturgical needs

Where the organ is placed is the single factor most critical to its success. The optimum location is one which allows the instrument to project its sound directly along the main axis of the nave. Any other location is a compromise.

Traditional placement is in the west gallery which has the added acoustical advantage of proximity to a hard ceiling surface as well as to walls and floor, all of which reflect and focus the sound of organ and choir in the direction of the listeners below. A gallery location also provides floor space for choir and instrumentalists, as well as for musical control by a conductor. It solves the liturgical problem of having musical forces front and center, allowing the organ case to be properly designed and ornamented without interfering with altar, lectern and clergy as visual centers for liturgical action. "A free standing position in the rear gallery is ideal, and in any case, an organ should stand as much in the open as possible, rather than being recessed in a chamber."[1]

Of course singers and other musicians are participants in the service, and it is inappropriate to try to hide them. In some instances, a location in front of the east wall will prove the right place. However, while satisfying requirements for projection of sound, this placement can lead to an over-simplification of the organ facade and an undesirable display of musical forces. If prior considerations dictate the location of choir and organ at the front of the nave, the liturgical implications of such a decision should be carefully considered.

1. In *Church Music And Theology*, SCM Press, London: 1959, p. 31.

1. Joint Commission on Church Music (c. 1958), as cited in Ochse, *The History of the Organ In The United States*, p. 410.

As to other locations, the effect of the organ, no matter how large or well-made, will be seriously mitigated if it must speak around corners or through obstructed openings. Planners of new instruments are well-advised to contemplate a smaller instrument and use funds which might provide a larger one to prepare a proper location, if none exists. For instance, many churches can accomodate a west gallery without extensive alteration of the rest of the nave. Responsible organ builders will give strong advice about location, often declining to build an instrument at all if it must be placed where it cannot sound well. They should be carefully attended.

Architectural problems

Among the worst possible solutions is to divide the organ in chambers on either side of the choir of the church. Since this has often been the case, especially with instruments installed before 1950, the thoughtful observer has good reason to ask why so many organs are placed in unsatisfactory locations. An immediate cause lies in the ease with which electric action organs were regularly disposed in illogical locations: placing the organ "where it would do the least harm architecturally — and the least good musically."[2]

A larger part of the explanation is found in the architectural design of churches constructed in the late nineteenth and early twentieth centuries under the influence of the English Tractarian Movement. Its effect was deeply felt in the United States, and the architectural results can be seen in the work of some of the most distinguished architects of that time, including Ralph Adams Cram, Bertram Goodhue, the Upjohns and many others. Many of these buildings, reviving medieval forms, are designed with great skill and integrity and constructed of natural materials. But, in almost every instance, the traditional free-standing location for the organ in a gallery (or on the choir screen, in some English churches) has been changed.

While the Tractarian movement raised liturgical awareness in admirable ways, its musical influence was disastrous, both for choirs and for organs. It assumed for parish churches the cathedral practice of antiphonal singing of the service from the choir with a minimum (in

2. As noted in the *Christian Science Monitor* for March 27, 1937 (in an article about the then new Germanic Museum organ at Harvard).

actual practice) of congregational participation. "Because of a misunderstanding of the makeup and function of the cathedral or collegiate choir, many churches in building or remodeling created a chancel placement for the choir (often divided into two sides). The resultant separation of the clergy from the people had harmful effects on the liturgy. Also, the choir was less able to give effective leadership to the people."[3]

Organs were relocated in the choir where they could not project into the church. By force of location, the divided choir sang to itself rather than to the congregation. Musical coordination required mirrors; illogical placement of singers, as well as organ, made control by a conductor almost impossible. It was, in fact, this attempt to give the altar central focus which created a cosmetic solution for music, rather than a genuine one. It went hand in hand with larger, louder organs and the increased use of anthems accompanied in the orchestral style.

The problems for organ design are well described by Clutton and Nilan in *The British Organ*[4]: "Generally parish churches fared worse than cathedrals. Organs were moved eastwards to accompany the newly robed choirs, and were re-erected, often considerably enlarged, in the chancels of side chapels never designed to hold them. The results were often tonally and architecturally deplorable . . . . This movement unfortunately coincided with the demand for the larger and louder organs deemed to be necessary to lead the singing of the nave congregations, and to accompany in quasi-orchestral style the increasingly elaborate choral services . . . . The larger the organs became, the more difficult it was to dispose of their more cumbersome parts. Consequently the various departments were stowed away in triforia, behind choir stalls, over vestries or sundry odd corners quite regardless of musical or visual effect."

Many fine buildings created during this time are in use in the United States. What then, can be done, when a new organ is planned for a church in which optimum placement is complicated by existing architectural features? First, the advice of an organ builder should be sought to find what is possible and desirable (musically and

3. M. Hatchett in *A Manual For Clergy And Church Musicians*, p. 31.

4. Batsford, London, 1963, p. 155.

liturgically) in such a building. Second, moving musical forces, including choir and organ, to some different location should be considered. For instance, shallow transepts in a resonant building might offer a reasonable compromise for placement if sound projection is both unobstructed and diffused by hard surfaces.

In some instances, when there is not sufficient height for a gallery, locating choir and organ at the west end of the nave is feasible. This requires floor space which does not inpinge on aisles and entries, nor unduly restrict congregational seating. Third, it is often wise to consider a smaller organ, which can be well located, rather than a larger one, if it must be placed where its sound cannot be directly heard. Fourth, when ceiling height permits, construction of a gallery at the west end of the nave (or in some cases, on a side wall) will be well worth the effort and expenditure.

What is the best acoustical environment?

Organ and choral sound; the spoken word

Organ and choral music require a more reverberant acoustical environment than some other types of music. The broad and diverse quality of organ sound, covering a wide spectrum of pitches, requires both substantial cubic volume and hard, reflective surfaces in order to develop fully. If both these requirements are not provided, a dull loudness results, rather than the bright, unforced quality which characterizes the organ at its best. It is this ability to envelop rather than overwhelm the listener with sound which is admired in the great instruments of Europe. Their sound is unquestionably enhanced by their acoustical environment which can be generally taken as optimum when a new environment is being created. These factors are relatively simple to describe, but realizing them in practical situations requires great persistence and care. The help of an experienced acoustical engineer should be obtained before any substantial work is undertaken.

Fear that clarity might be lost for the spoken word has often resulted in acoustics too dead for musical sound. It is clear that wise handling of acoustical factors can provide conditions where speech is clear and musical sound is not inhibited. More often than not, the solution involves proper placement of both speakers and musicians within a resonant building. Only in unusual situations will delayed amplification systems (for speech) be necessary. Even then, amplification should not be needed for music if instruments and singers are well located <u>and</u> well reflected.

Acoustical liveness is especially critical for good congregational singing. The advanced state of acoustical design now enables engineers and architects to remedy situations formerly thought to be hopeless. Carl Schalk has put the matter firmly and clearly: "What is often overlooked where choices between singing and speaking are suggested, however, is that a worship space sufficiently reverberant for spirited singing can easily be made suitable for public speaking. But a worship space designed only with the speaking voice in mind has effectively been ruined for the music-making of congregation, choir and organ. Since the people's song — whether hymns, psalms or liturgy — is such an important and vital ingredient in worship, it is not only natural but imperative that the public speaking voice accomodate itself to an environment that is sufficiently live for effective congregational song."[1]

Reverberation time

This is the elapsed time (in seconds) between the beginning of a sound and its decay. Reverberation varies according to pitch and intensity in a given space, and this is usually a desirable phenomenon. A well-proportioned room made of natural materials usually achieves its own appropriate reverberation. For instance, a small church seating only a hundred people cannot and should not give the same acoustical impression as a building of cathedral proportions. By the same token, smaller buildings require smaller organs which are scaled and voiced differently from instruments intended for larger spaces. In a church of moderate size, optimum reverberation time at mid-frequency pitch should approach at least two seconds when the building is comfortably filled with people.

Shape of space and cubic volume

Accoustical and architectural considerations are endemic to musical ones, and size is not always related to complexity. Total cubic volume

---

1. In "A Lament for resounding praise," *Christian Century*. Mar. 23-30, 1983.

is often more critical than square footage of floor space. Even though a small church may have minimal reverberation time, it can still be resonant. Generally, a simple, well-proportioned overall shape introduces fewer problems than a complicated one. The rectangular shapes of many Gothic and Georgian churches illustrate this ideal: they are rather long and high and relatively narrow. Even if ornament complicates surfaces, the overall shape itself may be relatively simple. Complicated configurations such as domes, tunnel vaults or segmented floor plans provide more areas for sound to "get lost" or be strangely reinforced in inconvenient places.

Excessive cubic volume is an extremely unlikely difficulty for most parish churches. The problem is usually the reverse: not enough cubic volume for musical sound to develop. Low ceilings are the most obvious culprit, even above a large floor space, since they limit total cubic volume.

Reflective surfaces

For efficiency, reflective surfaces must meet two criteria: they must be hard and they must be rigid. Masonry is an ideal reflecting surface and any material, including wood, softer than masonry is less efficient. Any material which absorbs water will also absorb sound, and such surfaces should be avoided in walls, ceilings and floors. This means that carpet and drapery are usually undesirable, especially in smaller buildings, as is any sound-absorbing synthetic tile. Wood and plaster surfaces should be hard; boards should be thick and tightly fitted since high frequencies are lost in cracks and other small apertures.

Such surfaces should have rigid backing since thin construction allows the material to dissipate bass frequencies by moving slightly when reflecting low pitches, thus absorbing rather than reflecting. Should a space be found too resonant, it is far better to modify it by using movable absorptive panels or drapery, etc., where needed, than to build in immovable absorption.

It is important to note that floor reflection is reduced as a building is filled with people. Pew cushions and kneelers are usually of less concern since they are covered by equally absorptive people.

Surfaces which appear to be reflective stone may in fact be absorptive. This is especially likely for churches constructed after the patenting of Akoustolith tile in 1916. Many great buildings of the early twentieth century used absorptive tiles, which had the appearance of other materials, to reduce reverberation for fear that speech would be unclear with the limited speech amplification systems then available. These tiles, which are amazingly strong and thin, are usually part of the structure of walls and ceilings and may be difficult to remove.

One way of restoring liveness to such surfaces is to cover them with several coats of an acrylic emulsion. A successful example of this treatment may be seen in the Duke University Chapel which has been transformed from a relatively dead room into " . . . a liturgical space without equal in the United States."[2]

An increasing number of churches, constructed during the period when "the basic acoustical design philosophy was 'deader is better,' "[3] have improved acoustics within existing spaces. At Saint Columba's Church, Washington, a false, sound-absorbing ceiling was totally removed when preparations for a new organ were made. At Saint Thomas' Church, New York, a treatment similar to that at Duke Chapel was employed to seal absorptive tiles.

Articulation of surfaces

While hard surfaces are essential to reflect sound, if the entire surface areas of walls and ceilings are totally uninterrupted, unpleasant *slapping* reflections or *dead* spots can result. This is usually prevented by articulations such as mouldings, window and door openings, beams or other natural irregularities. Avoiding perfectly parallel walls often helps prevent sonic focal points. Such lack of total symmetry can be observed in many early Gothic structures where a nave may not be perfectly straight or where other irregularities within an overall simple space have a favorable acoustical effect.

2.   Robert B. Newman and James G. Ferguson, Jr., *Gothic Sound for the Neo-Gothic Chapel of Duke University.* Boston: Bolt, Beranek and Newman, 1979.
3.   From an especially clear discussion of acoustical solutions in the American Guild of Organists Pamphlet, *Acoustics in Worship Spaces.*

What about the organ as architecture?

A good organ builder must have a good architectural sense. An organ inevitably becomes part of the building in which it is placed, and any attempt to disguise it is architecturally illogical and acoustically inhibiting. Wherever the organ is placed, it makes an inescapable architectural statement: it should neither merely call attention to itself (because of inappropriate ornament, size or location) nor deceive the viewer as to its size, function and resources.

Because the organ is a colorful and powerful instrument, its identity is not well served by excessively plain housing. Nor should it overwhelm the space in which it is seen and heard. As explained previously, a west gallery location for choir and organ is the best, both acoustically and liturgically, since it provides direct projection of sound, leaving the natural focus to altar and pulpit uncomplicated by musical forces. A location at the east end requires special care to avoid competing with altar and clergy.

Architects may be helpful in consulting with the organ builder, but they are not qualified to design the organ case whose proportions and facade are dictated by the resources inside the organ.

Once a liturgically and musically desirable location is found, the case and its facade should provide visual confirmation of the instrument's function and importance: essential, but not central.

While many considerations affect musical sound in a building, four primary factors should be a part of any architectural scheme for either new or rebuilt structures. These have been discussed above and are summarized below. Before proceeding to outline them, it is important to note that the organ case, which is a significant architectural contruction, must be designed by the organ builder, who should also consult with the architect. Compromise in any of the matters listed below will prejudice the best use of an organ, no matter how fine the instrument or the musician who plays it. These choices should never be left solely to the discretion of the architect who often may not agree that they are critical or who may feel forced to compromise in order to reduce construction costs. The essential matters are as follows:

Placement

Placement which allows sound to be projected directly to the hearers should be provided for organ and choir, preferably along the main east-west axis of the building.

Surfaces

Reflective surfaces of walls, ceiling and floor should be of hard materials (preferably plaster or masonry) with the necessary articulation (such as mouldings, window openings, etc.) to prevent concentration of sound at focal points.

Cubic volume

Large cubic volume is always preferable to less since it is essential to allow reverberation to develop. A low ceiling is the major culprit, especially in smaller buildings, since it reduces the total cubic space. Money saved by reducing volume is an unwise compromise because it precludes optimum development of musical sound, including congregational singing.

Shape of space

A well proportioned building produces a favorable sonic as well as architectural effect. "If it looks well, it will sound well" is a good maxim. This is borne out by countless early churches in Europe which tend to be quite high, rather narrow and long. In such buildings, constructed of reflective materials, musical sound is able to bloom without undue loudness. Structural obstructions should be zealously avoided around sources of musical sound. Lips of arches above a choir or organ gallery, for instance trap sound and prevent its even distribution.

When a building is acoustically healthy, no amplification should be needed for music, assuming that organ and choir are well placed. Speech reinforcement may be desirable in large spaces, but the need for a sound system for music usually is proof that fundamental acoustical and architectural factors have not been properly taken into account.

How is the organ best used?

Congregational singing and organ music

The two musical functions for which the organ is best suited are
supporting congregational singing and playing its own repertoire.
Imaginative playing of hymn tunes, exulting in the diversity of colors
inherent in the organ, can lead worshipers to participate with
heightened awareness and intensity. Any organ which cannot do this
(or any player!) is unworthy of the liturgy.

Pieces from the instrument's large and varied repertoire played before,
during or after a service provide occasion for thanksgiving and
meditation. As with no other instrument, the bulk of the organ's music
was created for liturgical use. It includes a host of works based on
familiar tunes, many of which have seasonal associations created by
centuries of use throughout Christendom. When the organ is used to
support singing of such tunes and to play music based on them, a
musical and liturgical unity of great power can result. This
combination of great music and its accessibility to a congregation
provides a unifying force for the worshiping community that is like no
other.

Improvisation

The elaboration of melodies from hymns or other sources is another
musical function for which the organ is well suited. A great tune in the
hands of a skilled improvisor can enhance service playing and provide
a way for quiet participation by the congregation. This venerable
tradition must not be confused with the compulsion to cover each
silent moment with pointless modulations or mindless musical
wallpaper, a practice more likely to distract the serious worshiper than
to be of help. Such ubiquitous use of musical resources destroys fertile
periods of silence and masks liturgical actions which require no
accompaniment. To use the organ for background music is to
prejudice its effect in more serious musical tasks. To design an organ
with this inappropriate function in mind is not only a waste of money
and effort, it can also compromise its ability to play a legitimate
repertoire.

Many church people, including Anglicans, have become accustomed to a school of service playing, based on instruments designed in an orchestral manner, located in remote parts of the building and provided with many soft effects. The popularity of such instruments earlier in the twentieth century is probably the main reason that the use of the organ for background music arose. Nonetheless, such practices are damaging to corporate worship because they encourage a private attitude and they destroy legitimate liturgical silences.

Choral accompaniments

Because its broad sound easily fills a large space, the organ is ideal for congregational support, and its variety of color makes it well suited to improvisation. For choral accompaniments in continuo style, it works well, as attested to by the large and excellent choral repetoire requiring such minimal support. It is less well suited, by nature and location, to intricate choral accompaniments, especially for works using transcriptions from orchestral scores. Also, when a choir sings well in tune, the sustained sound of the organ, regardless of its tuning, can cause intonation problems.

Because unwieldy transcribed accompaniments have been heavily used in the past, composers have often taken such unidiomatic writing as a norm: the organ is asked to perform as an orchestra, which is always unsatisfactory. Happily, there exists a vast body of liturgical music which is intended to be sung unaccompanied or which uses the organ only for continuo or in an idiomatic style.

Splendid unaccompanied music was produced by Elizabethan composers (Byrd, Gibbons Tallis, for instance) as well as by European composers. This tradition continues in the nineteenth and twentieth centuries in the music of Mendelssohn, Brahms, Poulenc and Vaughan Williams. The seventeenth and eighteenth centuries offer countless works which use the organ only for continuo, or as in many English verse anthems (Blow, Purcell, Boyce and Greene, for example) in an appropriate way. In the twentieth century, Britten's "Jubilate Deo," scored for SATB chorus and organ, exemplifies the success of a genuine organ part, as compared to a transcribed one.

It will sometimes be found desirable in large buildings with correspondingly large organs to provide a second "choir" organ of two to five stops which can be placed very near to singers and instrumentalists. This provides much better coordination for ensemble music than is likely with a large organ. Meanwhile, cantatas and oratorios by all means, but with instrumental rather than transcribed organ accompaniment!

New and old music

For parishes whose musical expectations have been formed under the influence of what might be called the large, loud but submerged organ, it is sobering to hear that a well-designed and carefully located instrument of 30 stops or less can have more versatility and presence than an organ twice its size designed in orchestral style and inhibited by unfortunate placement or acoustics. Progress towards honesty in organ design happily coincides with efforts to encourage liturgical participation by all.

It is this rediscovered identity of the traditional organ that makes it hospitable to new music written for it. Once again, composers are able to form a coherent idea of the resources offered by the instrument for which they write. That there has not been much new American organ music of quality is (as Walter Holtkamp noted, page 8) largely due to the fact that composers had lost interest in an amorphous and unpredictable instrument. A good organ should encourage parishioners not only to sing with joy but also to commission new music for it — preferably on an annual basis and, when possible, from competent local composers.

What about the organist?

Background and training

For organists, a good liturgical background is as important as an adequate technique. While a virtuoso keyboard facility is not required for much organ repertoire or for hymn playing, it is essential to remember that an organist's technique differs markedly from that of a pianist. A good pianist can certainly learn to play the organ relatively quickly, but the folk view of the organ as an instrument with several keyboards, playable by almost anyone, belittles the considerable experience needed for a decent musical result.

The best of organs can be made to sound unsatisfactory in the hands of an inept or unsympathetic player. And, conversely, a poor instrument often sounds deceptively fine when played by an experienced and sensitive musician. When a parish possesses a good instrument, however modest in size, it will do well to underwrite the costs of instruction for an organist so that the organ can be used to the best advantage. Organists who have been accustomed to electronic or electro-pneumatic instruments may be temporarily suprised by the simplicity which characterizes the traditional organ. The absence of aids to registration and even gadgetry associated with instruments dependent on electricity should not deter any musician equipped with a good pair of ears and reasonable understanding of the organ's varied repertoire.

Choosing organ music and improvising

Organists must be first of all be able to accompany congregational singing in an imaginative and rhythmic way. This requires the same knowledge of the organ's resources which playing organ music demands. Regarding the repertoire, players must be aware of its wide variety and especially of the existence of excellent music which is not inordinately difficult and which does not require a large organ for satisfactory performance. This substantial body of music, much of it suited to a single keyboard and only a few stops, can easily be overlooked if organ music is judged only in terms of a few familiar grand works. Music intended for virtuoso performance on large instruments actually forms the exception rather than the rule, and an overall understanding of the available repertoire is more important than a formidable technique.

Certainly the performance of larger works is appropriate on occasion and the ambitious organist will want to play them. Planning music to fit a given occasion is essential since music which merely calls attention to itself can create liturgical confusion if not chaos.

The ability to improvise, especially on melodies known to listeners, is an invaluable skill which requires considerable experience. Improvisation not only enhances understanding of the tonal colors of the organ, it also improves with practice. An organist of modest abilities should be encouraged to seek instruction in this skill along with other aspects of organ playing.

Consulting with planners

When a new instrument is planned, the organist is likely to have strong ideas about its design. When planners consult an incumbent musician (as they should do), they must also be aware that a good instrument will outlast any of them. As emphasized below (page 58), while the builder should listen carefully to the organist, advisor and to planners, the builder must nonetheless have the final word in the design of a new organ. The organist must understand that this is the only way to expect the best work from the builder, and all should remember that good instruments attract good musicians. Compromise or false economy at one point can be cause for repentance later.

How valid are different styles of design?

Individual styles

Modern organ builders create styles of organ building, usually based on one or more European styles, which characterize their individual work. The organ has assumed a somewhat different identity in each major European culture. In the classic period (c. 1650 to c. 1750), English, French, North European, Italian, and Spanish styles are readily distinguished, and the music of each region sounds best on its native instrument. Many changes came later, with the French romantic organ of the 19th century being the most clearly identified.

Whatever the differences among these styles, the presence of contrasted Principal choruses on each division of the organ was a common denominator. The organ's *Plein Jeu* is the *sine qua non* which identifies it: to a good builder, everything else is secondary. Beyond this, a judicious eclecticism may be employed, but the organ must still be designed as a unity; this is the real test of the organ builder. Speaking of traditional principles of organ building, the Dutch builder Flentrop states, "These principles require a definite unity in tonal technique and visual design. This means that together with designing the tonal structure, an architectural layout must be made according to the size of the building. The result is an organ in which every part is related to every other."[1]

---

1. D. A. Flentrop, "Behind the Pipes," The *Benjamin N. Duke Memorial*, p.15.

No matter how carefully an organ is designed, some music will have to be "translated" to fit it. The attempt to include components from all the major styles of organ building in one instrument produces an unwieldy and nondescript instrument, just as mixing Georgian, Romanesque and Gothic elements causes a building to be chaotic in appearance. A linguistic analogy makes this clearer: French, German or Spanish, spoken with an English accent may be quite understandable even though the pronunciation is not perfect. However, a paragraph switching abruptly from one to the other becomes unintelligible. The American all-purpose organ of the 1940's often exemplified this incoherence. It became so eclectic, especially in the case of large instruments, that coherence was sacrificed in the interest of variety.

All well-designed organs, in whatever style, are characterized by versatility sufficient to perform large segments of the organ repertoire assuming they are in the hands of a good musician. The built-in versatility is due more to the skills of builder and player than to an instrument's size. If the player does not understand the instrument, unmusical demands may be made upon it. For instance, the attempt to imitate the orchestra is always to some degree unsatisfactory, because it requires effects and sonorities alien to the organ.

Despite its size and complexity, a good organ is an intimate instrument: it responds to the wishes of a sympathetic player but it resists the unidiomatic demands of the inept. Just as a fine violin is not the best vehicle for music intended for the clarinet, so the best organ will literally balk — as though made of flesh and blood — when asked to play an accompaniment intended for the piano or a string quartet.

Classic, romantic, baroque, church or concert organs

Organ builders tend to avoid such terms as "baroque" or "romantic" because such designations have become both limiting and confusing. Both "classic" and "baroque" have been carelessly applied only to organs made in North Europe at some "early" period, or to attempts to copy such instruments, with varying degrees of success. "Romantic" is often used to mean "expressive," but only where nineteenth century music is concerned. These terms have lost their usefulness.

Reductive thinking overlooks the subleties inherent in any good design and ends up with stereotypes which no experienced builder would condone. A well designed organ will be "classic" in that it observes the basic principles common to all great instruments, not because it is limited to the music of one style or period. Conscientious builders accept these principles and make them their own by designing organs suited to the places in which they will be used. For amateurs to meddle in this technical area is presumptuous and dangerous. It is important for planners to recognize that any builder whose convictions can be dislodged by clients is unlikely to produce an instrument of integrity. "Find a trustworthy builder and then go home and pray," is the advice of one seasoned musician. Help in finding that builder could be one of the responsibilities of an advisor.

Finally, an important misconception which should be laid to rest once and for all is that church and concert organs constitute two different breeds. Probably users of such terms are thinking of small and large organs. Such a distinction can only have arisen from the supposition that "real" music has its place only in the concert hall and that liturgical music must be either bland or innocuous. Further, the same sounds which support congregational singing are essential to other organ music and vice versa.

When is it wise to rebuild an old organ?

Nineteenth century organs

Retaining a well-made 19th century organ is often a wise plan for both musical and historical reasons. Every effort should be made to salvage instruments by good builders, especially early ones and those which have important associations with a given parish. In the past, hundreds of viable organs have been discarded because no one took the trouble to see how they might continue. Often they were merely regarded as out of fashion. During the period before the revival of traditional organ building in the United States, electric action builders were reluctant to undertake repair or restoration of earlier instruments.

Also, in the past many builders did not consider using materials from an old organ in a new one because of the work hours required to adapt old materials to a new design. For instance, rebuilding a metal pipe requires taking it apart, resoldering it, perhaps reforming the mouth and lips, thereby consuming expensive shop time. However, with recent escalations in the cost of materials, including wood, tin and lead, reusing such materials can often make reductions in the cost of a new organ despite rising costs for labor. For instance, a modest saving can be effected by melting down old pipes considered unusuable so that metal can be recast. Large wooden pipes are often made of first quality pine, oak or maple which can be salvaged for new pipes or other needs.

A good organ builder's advice is the first essential in deciding whether an old instrument should be wholly or partly retained. If it is suitable in its original condition, so much the better. If not, the following factors should be considered:

Space Needs

American organs of the 19th century require more floor space than is ideal; even though traditional slider chests were used, design was not as compact as it might have been. Since it is expensive to alter chest layouts and actions, the builder's advice about space should be carefully heeded.

Reusing materials

When an older organ cannot be used *in toto*, it is often feasible to revoice existing pipes and retain one or more windchests with a new case and partially rebuilt action. Chests at least can often be reused but with new pipes and, therefore, with a new disposition prepared by the builder. A successful example of using new and rebuilt pipes, with an otherwise undistinguished organ, may be seen in the chapel of Virginia Theological Seminary.

Revising the disposition

Dispositions of many 19th century organs are limiting when present day musical needs are considered. Tonal design of that period often did not take into account a wide repertoire. Again, if mechanical parts of the organ are in good condition, a new dispostition might be created by the builder.

Electric action organs

In the case of older electric action organs, wooden parts and the pipes themselves are likely to be usable, but new windchests and action must be designed. Because of the need to replace electric or electro-pneumatic action parts after several decades, saving such an organ as a whole is likely to create recurrent financial problems (See also page 19). This is understandably traumatic, especially in a situation where there were conscientious efforts only a few decades earlier to acquire the best possible instrument. But it has been repeatedly demonstrated that where traditional organs have been chosen, they have not only musical advantages, but financial ones, as well: they last much longer and require less expensive maintenance.

However, there are instances where an electric action instrument has important historic value, giving importance of a different order to decisions about its preservation. In many cases, the best advice is to leave such an instrument *in situ*, if possible, while acquiring another, perhaps smaller, instrument for regular use. For example, an unaltered organ by E. M. Skinner, the most important American builder of his time, deserves more consideration for preservation than the work of lesser builders. Unfortunately this may not justify expenditures to make extensive repairs, especially considering musical and mechanical limitations. The responsible course is to respect the documentary importance of the instrument without being bound by it. Such decisions are painful to make, but continual refurbishing of a fundamentally "wrong-headed" instrument leads only to frustration and limiting of musical potential.

What are the major costs in building a new organ?

Labor and materials

Work hours constitute the largest part of the cost for building an organ, although rising costs for materials have contributed to increasing prices for instruments. Considerably more than half the total cost goes for labor, some of which is very specialized. It is essential that the builder in charge of the overall design supervise each aspect of its execution. Assistants skilled in drafting, joinery and cabinetry, pipe making, wood carving and leather work are also required. Although power tools are used, assembly line production methods are not appropriate to organ building. The person responsible for negotiating with the clients, as well as seeing to the design and its ultimate realization, must be intimately involved with each part of the process. Handwork is essential at every step.

The work hours required to produce an organ are astonishing. An organ of 20 stops can easily occupy the full time of a five-person shop for a full year, approximately 10,000 work hours! Nonetheless, it is easy to observe that organ builders rarely grow rich from their trade. When planners visit work shops, they would do well to note the standard of living of organ builders; it is usually more modest than that of the clients.

Design time

The builder must first design the entire instrument. This begins with taking measurements and making acoustical tests in the church. Then come hours of drawing board work, beginning with the laying out of the entire plan and continuing with drawing in the location for each pipe, valve, conductor, slider or other part of the mechanism inside the chest. Along with this, scales for all the pipes are determined and drawn in where applicable. The whole must take into account the overall floor plan, acoustics of the building, height, width and depth of the case, as well as the architectural appearance of the facade with its mouldings and other ornamentation. On occasion, drawings for parts of one instrument might be adapted for another similar one. Nevertheless, creating the overall design consumes many hours before actual construction can begin.

Windchests

Since windchests require many air-tight channels, all of which are fitted and glued by hand, their construction is especially demanding in time and competence. They also constitute a very expensive part of the total work. Although general price estimates may be made in terms of the cost per stop, this includes not only the pipes, but the chest and mechanism as well.

Key and stop actions

The action for both keys and stops consists of hundreds of moving parts which are made to operate with tiny clearances and to be as durable and trouble free as possible. If the organ must be awkwardly located or put into very limited spaces, costs for making a dependable key action will increase.

Pipes

To make metal pipes, raw metal is melted and cast into sheets, then hammered and/or planed and cut. The pieces are then formed around mandrels to make the proper shapes: usually cylindrical for the body of the pipe and conical for its foot. The parts are then soldered, and mouths and languids are formed for flue pipes according to their scale and the kind of sound desired. Reed pipes are fitted with reeds inside the boot at the foot of the pipe. All of these tasks are delicate and time-consuming, especially when it is remembered that an organ of only ten stops can easily have 700 pipes, each fashioned by hand.

Voicing is the operation in which pipes are placed on a windchest (called a *voicing table*) and regulated for pitch, loudness, tone quality and promptness of speech. The voicer may spend several days with only one stop. Reed pipes often consume large amounts of time since each reed tongue must be carefully shaped and adjusted. Final regulation, called finishing, of the entire organ occurs after it is set up in the church.

Case and carving

The organ case, made of hardwood panels, demands cabinetry of a high order. Depending on its size and ornamentation, it may be a major cost factor, especially if extensive carving is required.

The wind supply is often contained within the main case and includes a large bellows or reservoir with leathered folds, another costly item.

Installation

Depending on the size of the organ, a month or more is needed to erect the instrument in the church, make adjustments and complete the finishing. During this time two or more organ builders must be housed and fed: a good chance for the parish to offer hospitality to those whose work will become a part of their worship thereafter.

What is reasonable maintenance?

When the organ is new

A newly built organ requires a full calendar year to adjust to its environment. During the first year, especially when seasons change, adjustments and tuning may be needed frequently. This is normal for even the most stable instruments.

Thereafter the stability of the organ is directly related to fluctuations in temperature and humidity. The ideal climate for organs and other musical instruments is one which stays at 50% relative humidity and 70 degrees Fahrenheit. A good hygrometer and thermometer should be located inside the organ and checked frequently to monitor conditions. Regular full tuning and maintenance visits should be arranged for at least the end of autumn (when heat has been on for at least a week) and early summer (after heat is turned off). The tuner should be on call throughout the year for unexpected minor tunings and adjustments.

Humidity and temperature

Humidity affects especially the wooden parts of the organ which absorb or give up dampness and therefore shrink or expand slightly when humidity changes. This is most notable as heating begins in autumn when a comfortable humidity may be drastically reduced. Rising temperatures always dry out the air. When a significant change happens quickly (within 24 hours), wooden parts may warp or crack and serious damage can be done.

If interior humidity changes more than 20% during winter or summer, the organ builder should be consulted about providing extra humidification during winter. In poorly insulated buildings in cold climates, condensation of moisture may be a problem. If so, good engineering advice should also be solicited.

Temperature changes have immediate effect on tuning, especially on the metal pipes of the organ because they expand or contract as temperature rises or falls. Drastic changes in temperature will wreck the tuning of the whole organ with the reed pipes being most susceptible. The whole organ will be in tune only at the temperature at which the last tuning was done. If a building is heated or cooled only on Sundays, a <u>gradual</u> change in temperature is essential if the organ is to sound well. Under optimum conditions, it should return to its tuning after the room temperature returns to the same level at which tuning was done.

Tuning

Since tuning depends on both humidity and temperature, precautions should be taken in both winter and summer. In climates which are hot and damp during summer, air conditioning, which dehumidifies as well as cools, is very desirable. Its effect on the organ will be as salutary as it is on the parishioners.

Once the tuning temperature is reached, settling back into tune takes time. Care should be taken to see that the proper temperature is reached at least two hours before the organ is used and that the change occur as gradually as possible. If the organ has a swell box, shutters should be left open to allow circulation of warmer or cooler air.

The more stable the climate, the more stable the organ, whatever the season. Maintenance expense can be expected to increase in direct proportion to fluctuations in temperature and humidity.

Heating or cooling machinery should be carefully monitored for noise. Well designed fans, properly seated, can be silent; ducting can be baffled. If poorly designed, such equipment can cause annoying noise levels. This is not endemic and should not be tolerated.

Where to get advice?

Those charged with planning a new organ may well need outside guidance, especially as they begin. They may literally not know where to start. If so, an experienced advisor is needed.

Finding an advisor

Who should the advisor be? A person with broad liturgical as well as musical experience should be sought. Competence in identifying good workmanship is an equally important requirement. Often a musician whose parish has recently planned a new organ can be helpful. Another resource is the faculty of a music school or university where both organ instruction and liturgical practices are seriously taught. Seminary musicians can often be of assistance.

It is essential that an advisor be impartial as well as knowledgeable and not have a vested interest in only one builder. Clearly, any salesperson makes an unacceptable advisor. In fact, a firm large enough to employ salespeople is already too large for organ builders themselves to oversee all the important decisions required for design and construction of each instrument leaving the shop.

Advisor's function

The ultimate function of an advisor is to help planners find a competent and trustworthy organ builder. An earlier function is to help assess musical and liturgical needs, present and future. The advisor should also point out fundamental considerations, such as the importance of a live acoustical environment, proper location for the organ and its architectural impact on the interior of the church.

The advisor should help planners locate and inspect successful instruments by several makers and arrange visits to workshops of two or more makers. Such first-hand exposure is essential early on for education, especially when some planners may possess much interest but little experience. When visiting workshops or instruments, it is essential to have explanations about how the organ functions: to see where the wind supply is located, for instance, how many pipes actually are placed on a relatively small windchest, or how the keyboards are connected to the valves under the pipes. Such inspections remove much of the mystery about how an organ works and also show the intricate workmanship required to build it. Finally, the advisor should help planners in providing data to one or more builders so that they may submit clear proposals. If the builders asked to submit proposals are trustworthy, the advisor's task is ended.

Advice from the builder

Thereafter, design and construction of the instrument must be entrusted to the builder. The task of the advisor is to help less experienced people ask the right questions. Only an organ builder is fully competent to make a final design and provide details about an instrument's resources, space requirements and cost. If architectural changes in the building are involved, the builder should deal directly with the architect.

No one can really *supervise* a builder who has already been asked for the best of which the workshop is capable. This can result only when the builder is assured of the clients' confidence and respect.

Planners should be prepared for pressures from those with strong viewpoints, informed and otherwise, and they must beware of trying to pacify all shades of opinion; this can only lead to undistinguished results — the lowest common denominator being the most likely. Here again the builder's advice should be carefully considered at each step of the process.

Those who wish to inform themselves in more detail should consult one or more of the publications found in the resource list at the end of this book. This list includes works with information in a form accessible to readers without extensive experience. They are available from publishers or most libraries. Although technical language accompanies detailed descriptions, perusal of such readings will extend the beginner's understanding of the organ and its history.

How best to negotiate with the organ builder?

While an organ builder is being chosen, and especially after this choice is made, planners will be asked to provide a variety of musical, liturgical, architectural and acoustical information to enable the builder to come to the best possible solution. Those charged with providing information will also have many questions for the builder. Both sides of the negotiating table will find their tasks easier if the needed information is provided accurately (including measurements of spaces in the building) and as early in the process as possible. Unique situations will always produce unique questions, but in general, the following two lists should be helpful:

Information needed by the builder

Regarding space and placement of the organ and choir:

Drawings showing floor space and height in the building should be provided. Although builders usually make their own measurements of critical areas, a full set of drawings giving structural, electrical, heating and air conditioning details is very desirable. Square footage is important not only for the space occupied by the organ, but also for choir and other musicians.

Any architectural features or liturgical appointments which would be difficult or undesirable to alter should be pointed out. The relation of the location of organ and choir to congregation and liturgical action should be carefully considered. This is a point at which the builder's experience should be solicited as it might produce useful advice.

Regarding acoustics:

A description of all surfaces (walls, floors, ceilings) in the church should be provided. Information concerning thickness of wall and ceiling facings will also be important since thin plaster or paneling without rigid backing reflects sound inefficiently. Any areas covered with carpet or other absorptive materials should be pointed out.

Regarding temperatures and humidity:

The builder will want to know what, if any, extremes of temperature and humidity occur as seasons change and what kinds of controls, if any, exist for controlling these factors.

Regarding appearance of the organ:

While good builders will design an organ case to fit visually in its new environment, any symbols appropriate for carvings in the organ facade and important to a particular parish should be described.

The appearance of the organ can be drastically affected by structural complications in the building, chiefly windows. If the builder feels that optimum projection of sound requires that the organ be placed in front of existing window openings, this advice should be very carefully considered. While it is possible to produce case designs which do not obscure existing windows, this often produces a less graceful case and may increase costs.

Information needed by planners

Regarding preparation of space:

The following eventualities should be clarified:

Will platforms or floors need to be altered in advance in order to provide not only for the organ but also for singers and instrumentalists? Should any construction (such as a new gallery) be considered? Are there sound absorbing surface materials which ought to be removed and replaced with reflective surfaces? Are sources of heat or air conditioning too near the organ, thus affecting tuning? Does the space get direct sunlight which can warm part of the organ, throwing it out of tune? What lighting alterations are needed?

Regarding delivery time and payments:

The builder should provide a clear schedule of financial arrangements, but the following questions should be considered:

How long will construction of the organ take and when can delivery be expected?

How much time will be needed in the church for final setting up and finishing?

How many workers, if any, will require housing and food and for how long?

What kind of warranty is the builder prepared to give?

When does the instrument become the insurance responsibility of the parish?

Regarding the builder's experience:

Where did the builder learn the trade: with whom was an apprenticeship served?

Where might other work by the builder be inspected and how may recommendations be obtained?

And finally, who will maintain the organ after it is installed? Can this be done by the builder or are there recommendations for a firm nearer by?

Resource List

The following brief list includes sources which should be readily available in a good library or directly from the publishers. For those who wish to read further, most include extensive bibliographies, and many are profusely illustrated.

Committee on Acoustics and Architecture (American Guild of Organists), *Acoustics in Worship Spaces*, 815 Second Avenue, New York, NY 10017.

Blanton, Joseph, *The Organ in Church Design*, Albany, TX: Venture Press, 1956.

Douglass, Fenner, *et al*, *The Benjamin N. Duke Memorial*, Durham, NC: Duke University, 1976.

Fesperman, John, *Two Essays on Organ Design* Raleigh, NC: Sunbury Press, 1975.

Hatchett, Marion J., *A Manual for Clergy and Church Musicians,*, New York, NY: The Church Hymnal Corporation, 1980.

Harvard Dictionary of Music, "*Organ*" article, Cambridge, new edition in press.

New Grove Dictionary of Music and Musicians, "*Organ*" article, London: MacMillan, 1980.

Newman, Robert, and Ferguson, James *Gothic sound for the neo-gothic chapel of Duke University*, Cambridge, MA: Bolt, Beranek and Newman, Inc., 1979.

Ochse, Orpha, *History of the Organ in the United States,* Bloomington, IN: Indiana University Press, 1975.

Owen, Barbara, *The Organ in New England*, Raleigh, NC: Sunbury Press, 1979.

Pape, U., *The Tracker Organ Revival in America*, Berlin, Pape Verlag, 1978.

Williams, Peter, *A New History of the Organ*, Bloomington, IN: Indiana University Press, 1980.

Wilson, Michael, *Organ Cases of Western Europe*, Montclair, NJ (36 Park St.): Abner Schram, 1979.

For publications of the Organ Historical Society

Address the Society at
Box 26811, Richmond, Virginia 23261

For information regarding nineteenth century organs for sale

Address The Organ Clearing House
Alan Laufman, *Director*
Box 104, Harrisville, New Hampshire 03450

For publications of the Association of Anglican Musicians

Address the current president of the Association.

Official publication of the American Guild of Organists

The American Organist
815 Second Avenue
New York, New York 10017

Appendix

How to proceed: A guide for planning sessions

The following steps may be helpful to a group considering a new organ. Planners should expect that their task will be time-consuming and should allow at least six months to gather information and make a recommendation to the Vestry.

The number and order of sessions can be arranged to suit local requirements and the experience of those involved. A chairman or other person should prepare a clear and limited agenda for each meeting. All concerned should read the four sections of the text before beginning, and refer to them as suggested below.

Session I

Review musical and liturgical needs along with the rector and parish musician.

Clarify why an organ is desired and how it will be used.

REVIEW IV, *pages 29-34 and 46-48.*

Session II

Decide how to prepare the congregation for receiving an organ.

Make a tentative schedule for progress and issue progress reports as appropriate. Include plans for funding the organ.

Decide if outside advice is needed. If so, secure an advisor. Carefully define the advisor's role in advance. Negotiate with advisor regarding fees.

REVIEW IV, *pages 54-60.*

Sessions III-VI and as needed

Arrange to visit three or more successful recent organs by different builders, and the workshops of two or more builders.

Ask questions about how organs work and about the reliability of each instrument. Observe the quality of the workmanship, including cabinet work, case ornamentation and architectural appearance, as well as the sound of the organ.

REVIEW III, *pages 11-23.*

Session VII

Consider the building into which the organ is to go, with attention to:

> Liturgical and musical functions,
>
> Architectural appearance and carvings for facade,
>
> Placement,
>
> Acoustical environment,
>
> Temperature and humidity conditions.

REVIEW IV, *pages 34-37 and 44-45.*

Session VIII

Assemble information to send to two or more builders, asking them to visit the church, meet with the committee and then submit proposals. Include a general statement of the need as viewed by the committee, and the following:

> Drawings of the building, showing structural, electrical and cooling/heating designs,
>
> Notations describing any liturgical or architectural factors affecting appearance or location of the organ,
>
> Estimate of projected funding for an organ.

Sessions IX-XI and as needed

Meet with each builder to review proposals submitted.

Ascertain each builder's recommendations as to:

> Optimum size for an organ,
>
> Optimum location in the building,
>
> Acoustical problems needing attention,
>
> Temperature and humidity conditions,
>
> Payment schedules and warranty,
>
> Maintenance of the organ.

REVIEW IV, *pages 50-52, 57-58 and 60-62.*

Final Session(s)

Evaluate proposals and make recommendations to Vestry.

REVIEW II, *page 6.*

Glossary

Technical terms which appear in the text are defined in the following list.

action　The mechanical connection between keys and pipes (key action) or between the stop knob and the mechanism for turning a stop on or off (stop action).

celeste　An organ voice consisting of two pipes for each note with one tuned slightly flat to produce an undulating effect.

chorus　The combination of all the pitches within one tone family.

combination action　A device for turning on or off several stops at once.

console　A collective term describing the keyboards and stop controls for an organ. *Synonym*, keydesk.

coupler　A mechanical device for connecting one keyboard to another.

disposition　The list of stops in the entire organ; or, the way stops are disposed over several keyboard divisions.

division　A self-contained part of the organ consisting of its own windchest, pipes and keyboard. For instance, Great, Positive, Swell or Pedal.

flue stop　An organ stop whose pipes produce sound by wind passing through a flue, which is an opening between the upper and lower lips of the pipe. *Flute* and *Principal* sounds use flue pipes, which make up the majority of pipes in the organ. *See also*, reed stop.

flute stop　An organ stop with flue pipes of relatively wide scale producing tone known as "flute sound," with less harmonic development than Principal tone. Flute pipes are often closed at the top.

keydesk　The part of the organ containing the keyboards and stop knobs. *See also*, console.

manual   A keyboard played by the hands.

mixture   An organ stop consisting of two or more pipes for each note sounding pitches at the octave and fifth above unison pitch.

organ case   The wooden housing around the entire organ or around one or more divisions of the organ.

pedalboard   An organ keyboard, usually of 30 to 32 notes, beginning at low C and played by the feet.

pipe shades   The ornamental carving placed around the tops of pipes in the facade of an organ.

Plein Jeu   The full sound of the organ, consisting of the Principal chorus or all pitches of the Principal family of tone.

principal chorus   The combination of all the pitches of the Principal family on a division of the organ.

principal stop   An organ stop, with open flue pipes of relatively narrow scale, producing the most characteristic organ tone called "Principal sound." *See also*, flute, reed.

reed stop   An organ stop, whose pipes produce sound from a vibrating metal blade or "reed," rather than by passing wind through a flue, as in other organ pipes.

register   *See*, stop.

scaling   The measurement of the diameter of a pipe. "Principal" pipes have narrow scales or thin diameters, while "Flute" pipes have wider scales. Scales can also affect loudness as well as quality of sound; hence a good builder scales differently for buildings of different sizes and acoustical properties.

stop   A group of pipes, one for each key, which can be made to sound or be silenced by moving the stop knob to on or off position. *Synonym*, register.

swell box   An enclosure, usually wooden, around a windchest and its pipes, with louvers at the front, which can be opened or shut to increase or decrease volume.

swell division   A division of the organ consisting of windchest and its pipes located inside a swell box.

tremolo, tremulant   A device which causes regular small pitch variations by exhausting small amounts of air from the organ's wind supply, producing a vibrato effect.

unison pitch   "Normal" sounding pitch; for instance, the same pitch as the piano. An open pipe, eight feet long will produce unison pitch at low C. Organ stops at unison pitch are marked, 8'; those an octave higher 4', etc.

unit organ, unified organ   An electric action organ in which a set of pipes is made to sound at two or more different pitches, in lieu of having a separate set of pipes for each stop.

voicing   The regulation of a pipe's speech and tone quality. This is done by making delicate adjustments at the mouth and the foot of the pipe, to control the flow of wind inside the pipe.

windchest   A box (literally a chest) of wood, with air tight joints, having holes bored in its top, over which rest the pipes of the organ. Each division of the organ has its own separate windchest.

About the author

John Fesperman is curator of musical instruments at the
Smithsonian Institution and organist of Grace Church
in Washington, D.C. Before coming to Washington, he
was Director of Music at Christ Church, Boston and a
member of the faculty of both the New England
Conservatory and Boston University. He also worked
for a short time in the shop of Charles Fisk.

As a student of organ playing and organ design, his
most recent contributions have been *Organs in Mexico*,
based on Smithsonian fieldwork in Mexican colonial
centers, and *Flentrop in America*, an account of the
Dutch organ builder D.A. Flentrop's work in the United
States. His earlier recordings include choral works of
Monteverdi, Bach, Gibbons and Schütz, and organ
music of Couperin and de Grigny; awaiting release is a
record of the Fisk organ in Mount Calvary Church,
Baltimore, including music of Copland, Brahms and
earlier composers.

His first serious musical employment was as
organist of the Chapel of the Cross in Chapel Hill, while
a student at the University of North Carolina. He has
been involved with liturgical music ever since.

July, 1984